P\
PLATEAU ᴛᴏ PINNACLE

"Plateau to Pinnacle *takes the business parable to a whole new level. The story will hit home with every financial advisor and the chapter to-do lists are fantastic. They lay out exactly what you need to do to systematize every aspect of your business.*"
— **Stuart, Vice President, Portfolio Manager, Financial Advisor, Retirement Income Certified Professional, Honolulu, HI**

"*If you're serious about taking your business to a new level, you have to read this book. The story keeps you moving through the book quickly and if you take the time to develop and implement the 9 Secrets, success will be yours.*"
— **Aimee, Senior Vice President, Ponte Vedra Beach, FL**

"*The 9 Secrets are systems every advisor knows they should have, and wishes they did have in their business. It's the storytelling and the way the content is presented in* Plateau to Pinnacle *that motivates you to actually do it. It can be a career changing book.*"
— **Cindy, Vice President, Financial Advisor, Chartered Retirement Planning Counselor, Visalia, CA**

"*Tamberella and Wright's knowledge and experience in the business are evident throughout the entire book. They obviously know just what it takes to be successful in the business.*"
— **Michael, CFP, Financial Advisor, Santa Barbara, CA**

PLATEAU *to* PINNACLE

PLATEAU *to* PINNACLE

9 SECRETS OF A MILLION DOLLAR FINANCIAL ADVISOR

A BUSINESS PARABLE

ERIN TAMBERELLA

with contributions by Rick Wright

Mill City Press, Minneapolis

To Caleb my son, the joy of my life and the most avid reader I know — you inspire me every day to be the best I can be. I hope this book inspires you.

To my Mom and biggest fan — your unconditional love, support and belief made it all possible.

"Whether you think you can or you think you can't – you're right."

– Henry Ford

CONTENTS

PREFACE

This is a book for financial advisors. It's intended to lead you through a step-by-step process for systematizing the most important aspects of your business. Regardless of production level, every advisor recognizes the need to have clearly defined, repeatable systems in place in order to grow and break through the inevitable plateaus inherent in the business.

After 17 years as a financial advisor, 3 years as a branch manager, and 10 years as a coach, I know from experience that the earlier in your career you build these systems, the faster your business will grow. Most importantly, these systems give you the ability to leverage your existing book for increased assets, referrals, and revenue.

I've had the privilege of coaching hundreds of financial advisors from all over the country, from all different firms, and at all different production levels. Developing systems and a scalable process for business is a universal need and desire among advisors.

Although building systems for your business is essential to your growth, it's not the most exciting thing you'll ever do in your career. That's precisely why I chose to write this book as a story rather than a step-by-step manual.

This book is the story of a fictitious financial advisor named Luke who, through a series of unfortunate events, meets an extremely knowledgeable but mysterious mentor by the name of Victor Guise. Victor leads Luke through building the systems he must have in place to reach his goal of becoming a million-dollar producer. Along the way, Victor teaches Luke some life lessons as well.

Although Luke is fictitious, he has a little bit of all my clients in him. His problems and issues are the ones I hear every day as an executive coach. Victor's wisdom is the culmination of all I have tried to give to my clients over the years, as well as all I've learned from them.

My suggestion would be to enjoy the story and use the Chapter To-Do lists at the end of each chapter as your step-by-step guide for building the system discussed in that chapter. The "Putting It All Together" chapter at the end contains a comprehensive guide to the lessons outlined throughout the course of the book.

At the end of each session with Victor, Luke receives a packet with additional resources in it. Some of the contents of Luke's packets can be found by following the link referenced in the "Additional Resources" section of the book.

Further resources to help you on your own journey to success are available at www.executivetransformations.com .

Erin Tamberella
info@executivetransformations.com

ACKNOWLEDGMENTS

First and foremost, my sincerest thanks goes to my business partner and contributor, Rick Wright. Without him, this book would have never happened. It would still be just another item on my bucket list. Throughout the project, he had the instinctive ability to know exactly when to push, back off and encourage. His honesty, insight and contributions made what seemed impossible, possible. These are precisely the characteristics that make him such a talented coach and awesome business partner.

Thanks to all the financial advisors I've had the honor of coaching over the last 11 years. I've gained tremendous insight and knowledge from each and every one of you.

A very special thanks goes to my client and friend, Helene Botos who was the very first financial advisor to read the rough draft of this book and give me the thumbs up. You're an incredible client, great friend and constant source of inspiration to me.

To Andy Baggs, Neil Powell, Bill Dixon, you are my "stars" and watching you guys grow as financial advisors to the level you are now has been incredibly fulfilling, given me great satisfaction and complete confidence in the systems I present in the book. Thanks for letting me be a part of your tremendous success.

To all the advocates I have as clients, thank you for

believing in me and in this project. I'd like to give a special thanks to Gina Hill who never failed to ask me about the book every single week in our coaching sessions. Your genuine interest and concern encouraged me more than you will ever know.

A special thanks must go to Cindy Myers who has the dubious distinction of being my very first coaching client and remains one to this day. It has been a real privilege to coach you and watch you grow.

To everyone at *Horsesmouth* but especially Doug Pierce, you have been instrumental in building my writing and coaching career. Thank you Doug, for discovering my writing, giving me my first professional validation as a writer and being such as strong advocate for many years.

To Jill Cheeks my writing coach at Mission Marketing Mentors, your eternal optimism, belief and direction in navigating the many essential steps in going from idea to actual book proved invaluable. Thank you for your support and expertise.

Thanks to Mark Levine and everyone at Mill City Press. You took a total "out of my comfort zone" experience and put me back there for what's been a virtually seamless process.

A very special thanks to my entire editing team. In my mind, it definitely takes a village to edit a book. Thanks for your sharp eye to detail, maintaining my sense of perspective and allowing me to ultimately produce a content-rich book while maintaining the integrity of my characters.

To Jason Sutton, who has been my "Victor" in life and health. Thanks for changing my life, and me in the process. You never gave up on me and for that I will always be grateful. You are a true friend and confidante.

Mom, thanks for supporting me in every way possible through this project and throughout my entire life. Thanks for your unwavering belief in my potential, for always maintaining a sense of humor and helping me to maintain mine, regardless of the circumstances.

A huge thanks to you Caleb for giving up so much of your Mom time so that this book could be possible. Thanks bud, for allowing me to live my dream and for sharing every milestone with me along the way. There's no one I'd rather share this with than you.

Finally, I thank God for making everything possible with just a little faith.

PROLOGUE

I remember exactly what I was doing the night we got the call. They say life can turn on a dime, and that night it did.

Everyone else described it as a blur, but not me. I remember every detail as if the rest of the world had just stopped. It was Tuesday night. Maya was already sleeping, and Aimee had just begun her evening beauty ritual.

Ethan and I were lying across his bed as I drilled him on multiplication tables. We'd just finished 9 x 9. I'd shown him my trick for the nines, and he was starting to get the hang of it.

He crinkled his nose and squinted his big brown eyes. This was obviously the sign of intense concentration in a 10-year-old. "Wait, Dad, I think I got it," he said with his usual eager-to-please excitement. "We're multiplying 9 times another 9, so it's gotta start with an 8."

"Good," I encouraged.

"And 8 + 1 = 9. So 81! The answer's 81, Dad!" he squealed.

"Awesome, buddy. I think you've got it now!" I was as excited as he was. Finally, we'd conquered the nines.

I heard the phone ring down the hall. We were one of the last families I knew who still paid for a landline even though we all had cell phones. It was a retro thing I guess. Anyway, I remember Aimee answered on the third ring.

"Time for bed, bud. Go brush your teeth," I ordered, trying to extract myself from his bed. Ethan's bed was way too soft, but he liked it that way. I, on the other hand, felt like I was fighting my way out of quicksand every time I had to climb out of it. Note to self: next time sit at the desk.

Suddenly, Aimee burst through the door, our white Lab, Charlie, barreling in behind her. Sobbing, she collapsed into my arms, shaking uncontrollably. My first thought was that someone had died.

Aimee and I had been together since college and had been married for 18 years. She was my rock, and to see her hysterical unnerved me. I guided her over to the bed and sat next to her. I pushed her auburn hair away from her face and tried to gently wipe away her tears with my thumb, but they just kept coming.

"I'm going to get you some tissues. Take deep breaths and I'll be right back, okay?"

She nodded as she gasped for breath in between sobs. I rushed into the bathroom that Ethan shared with Maya. Charlie followed right on my heels. Ethan stood frozen, purple toothbrush in his hand and panic on his face. "What's the matter with Mom," he whimpered.

"I don't know, bud, but I need you to let Charlie out for me. He's got to go." I thought it best to give Ethan a job while I found out what was going on.

"Is she going to be okay?"

"She'll be fine," I reassured him.

"Why is she so sad?"

"I don't know, Ethan, but I need you to take care of Charlie for me," I said firmly.

He stared at me for several seconds and then grabbed Charlie by the collar. Avoiding the doorway to his room, he dragged the big dog out through the hallway. "C'mon, Charlie."

I snatched the box of tissues off the counter and rushed back to Aimee. Tears still poured down her cheeks, but at least her breathing had steadied. She plucked several tissues from the box and wiped her puffy green eyes. She took my hand in hers.

"What's going on, babe?" I asked softly. "Is it your grandmother?" Aimee's grandmother had broken her hip in a fall last year. Since then, it had been one health issue after another. The two were very close, and Aimee visited her every week.

Her eyes met mine, and she shook her head sadly. "There's no easy way to tell you this, Luke." Her tears started flowing again. "It's Ben. He had a heart attack tonight." She paused and then whispered, "He's dead."

I heard her words but couldn't comprehend them. Ben and I had been best buds since the sixth grade. Our friendship was the only reason I'd survived middle school, and in high school, we'd played football together. He was the big, gregarious defensive end, and I was the tall, skinny wide receiver. Thirty years later, Ben's dad still called us Laurel and Hardy.

We'd graduated from college together, and both became financial advisors. We'd even started in the same training class at Strong Hauser. From the beginning, we knew we'd be business partners. Most people thought we already were. But we decided early in our careers that we each had to make it on our own first. It had taken us 10 long years at the firm, but now the partnership agreement was at the region, awaiting final approval.

We'd made reservations at the girls' favorite restaurant on Friday night to celebrate. Ben's parents, Joe and Betty, were throwing a big party for us on Saturday night. It was supposed to be a great weekend.

We were the same age, for god's sake! We were best man at each other's weddings. Our kids were less than a year apart. Aimee must have misunderstood. There had be some kind of a mistake.

"Luke!" Her voice seemed far away. "Luke, are you okay?" I just stared at her, unable to speak. I felt cold, very cold—like all the blood was being sucked out of me. Thousands of black spots suddenly clouded my vision.

"You don't look so good, Luke. Lie down," I heard Aimee say.

She fluffed Ethan's black and blue Batman pillows and then eased me down onto his bed. "Uh, are...are you sure?" I stammered.

Aimee squeezed in next to me. "Cindy just called. She was still at the hospital with Joe. Betty's with the kids."

Ben and Cindy had been married almost as long as we had. What was Cindy going to do? She hadn't worked since the twins were born. Ben had some life insurance, but I didn't know how much, and the kids were only nine years old. I knew Ben's parents would help. Joe had sold part of his shipping business a couple of years ago, so they had money. They loved Cindy and adored the twins, but I couldn't begin to imagine how tough it was going to be—for everybody.

I closed my eyes and let the tears stream down my face. I didn't even try to stop them. "Cindy and the kids..." A voice that I barely recognized as my own trailed off. "He just dropped me off to pick up my car not three hours ago. How... How can he be dead?"

"I don't know, honey. I just don't know," she mumbled and squeezed my hand.

My mind drifted back to the afternoon, scanning my memory for anything out of the ordinary, any warning sign I should have noticed that may have saved his life. As usual, we'd gone to the gym when we left the office. Ben was laughing and joking just like he always did.

He was excited about the partnership. We both were. We'd been meticulously planning it out for months—our roles and responsibilities, how we'd cross-pollinate our books, how we'd handle new business. We were ready. We'd signed the partnership agreement last week.

Then it hit me. "I should have known," I groaned.

Aimee turned to look at me. "What are you talking about?"

"This afternoon when we left the gym, Ben said he was tired, and he asked me for a Tums. He said he had heartburn and blamed it on the meatball sandwich he had for lunch. Heartburn, Aimee! I could have saved his life if I'd just been paying attention!"

"Don't be ridiculous, Luke. There's no way you could have known. Nobody could have. Just because someone says they're tired or asks for a Tums doesn't mean they're about to have a heart attack. You're not going to blame yourself for this, so just stop it. Now!"

Her tone told me not to argue. We lay there in silence. I heard Ethan and Charlie downstairs in the kitchen.

"You know the last thing he said to me?" I asked softly.

"No. What did he say?"

"When we left the gym, the traffic was terrible on the way to pick up my car. When we finally got to the dealership, I told him I really appreciated him dropping me off, and he said—"

"Pay it forward," Aimee said with a faint smile.

Pay it forward…That's what Ben always said instead of "You're welcome." It was one of his favorite expressions.

"I can't believe he's gone." My eyes burned, the tears overflowing onto my cheek. "I should probably go over there and be with them."

Aimee nodded and then sighed heavily. "Luke, we have to tell the kids."

I'd already started fighting my way out the quicksand bed. "Tomorrow. Let's wait until tomorrow."

I shuffled down to our bathroom and splashed some water on my face. I felt like I'd aged 10 years in the last 30 minutes, and when I stared at the tired, splotchy face in the mirror, I looked it. Already, I felt a void I knew would never go away.

My life was about to change. At that moment, there was no way I could have known just how much.

1. THE MEETING

"Sometimes it's the smallest decisions that can change your life forever."
                                        – Keri Russell

Ben was dead. He was my best friend and business partner, and now he was gone. Well, technically, I didn't know if we were business partners or not. We'd signed the partnership agreement but hadn't gotten final approval before the heart attack. Who knew how the firm would decide to handle that?

It was the day after his funeral, and tonight, his parents were hosting a party to celebrate his life. Joe and Betty were both Irish, and evidently that's what they do when someone dies. Friends, family, and a lot of big-money people Joe knew from his business were all going to be there. Originally it was supposed to be a party to celebrate the partnership. Now we were saying good-bye to Ben. It still didn't seem real to me.

"I don't feel much in the party mood," I announced to Aimee.

She walked out of the bathroom, mid-makeup, looking as radiant as ever. Aimee was striking, with silky auburn hair and

1

big green eyes that always seemed to be smiling. I knew no one would notice the sadness in them tonight. No one but me.

"C'mon, Luke. This is for Ben. According to Joe and his Irish tradition, yesterday was the day of mourning. Tonight is a night of celebration," she declared, hands on her hips.

"I'm not Irish."

"Tonight you are," she said sternly as she fiddled with my tie.

"How do you know so much about Irish tradition anyway?"

"Google." A crooked smile spread across her face. Something about that smile made everything better, even tonight.

She continued in a know-it-all tone usually reserved for the kids. "Tonight we're *celebrating* Ben. Everyone is supposed to laugh and tell their own stories about him. It's going to cheer you up."

I just grunted and flopped down on the bed. She gave me a kiss on the cheek before disappearing into the bathroom to finish getting ready. I stared up at the ceiling fan circling above me. *The circle of life,* I thought. Nothing was going to cheer me up—nothing short of seeing Ben alive and well again, but I guess at this point, that would just freak me out. I sighed heavily.

Aimee was ready in no time, one of her many endearing qualities. I didn't feel much like talking in the car, but I admired Aimee's attempt at upbeat conversation. She even managed to coax a couple of smiles out of me along the way.

Cars lined both sides of the street several blocks before we even turned onto Joe and Betty's street. I knew they were all there for Ben. Lucky for us, Joe had saved us a spot in his garage. Before I knew it, we were standing at their front door.

"You can do this," Aimee said in her most reassuring voice.

"Thanks, babe." I hugged her and rang the doorbell.

From outside, it sounded like a regular party. I could hear people talking and laughing. Maybe Aimee was right. Maybe it would cheer me up.

We waited several minutes, but no one answered. Finally, I turned the handle and walked in like I used to when I was a kid. The house was packed, almost to capacity. I heard Joe's roaring laughter coming from the general area of the den. I grabbed Aimee's hand and began navigating my way through the crowd to the back of the house.

I knew almost everyone there, so we moved slowly. People stopped us every few steps to offer their condolences. Finally, as I was just about to reach the den, I ran right into Dan Chapman, the manager of our branch. I hadn't been in the office since Ben died.

"Luke," he said, shaking my hand. "You're just the man I've been looking for. Can I borrow him a second, Aimee?"

Dan was a good guy and tried to look out for his advisors as much as he could in a large firm. Aimee smiled politely and let go of my hand. "He's all yours," she said and set off on her own, continuing her journey to the back of the house.

Dan pulled me into the hallway where it was less crowded. Only a couple of people stood fidgeting in front of the bathroom door.

"First of all, Luke, I'm really sorry about Ben. I know how close you two were."

"Thanks, Dan." I concentrated on keeping my voice steady and swallowing the lump that was growing exponentially in my throat.

He paused, avoiding my eyes. I knew it wasn't going to be good news. "This probably could have waited until Monday, but I wanted to give you time to process it. I talked to the region today and with Ben." He cleared his throat before continuing. "Uh...Ben's death...they can't approve the partnership agreement."

"I didn't really expect them to," I replied.

"I'm going to have to distribute his accounts on Monday according to the production averages. Of course, I'm going to pull 'manager' and give you the family accounts. I need you to make a list of people you know personally in his book, and I'll see what I can do."

"Whatever," I answered flatly. "The last thing I feel like doing is scavenging through my dead friend's accounts." I coughed, hoping it would dislodge the lump in my throat. I didn't know how much longer I could hold back my tears.

"I know, I know. Look, I can't even imagine how hard this is on you, but Ben," he paused, "he'd want you to have them all. So at least look through them and give me something to work with. You have a list, right?"

I sighed. I knew he was just trying to help, but I didn't know if I could deal with the accounts right now. "I'll try," I muttered. "Is that it?"

"Not exactly, Luke."

I didn't like the seriousness in his tone. "What?"

"It's about Cindy," said Dan, shifting his weight.

"What about Cindy," I barked. Suddenly, I felt the overwhelming need to protect Ben's family.

"Ben never signed the FFASA form."

"What the hell is that, Dan?" I asked. I could feel my blood pressure rising.

"It's the Family Financial Advisor Succession Agreement. That's the form that provides Cindy with revenue from Ben's book for the next five years. He never signed it."

"What are you talking about?" I demanded. My face burned, and I knew I was talking louder than I should.

"In order for Cindy to get a five-year revenue stream off of Ben's book, he has to have signed the form, and he didn't. So we can't pay her out. She's not going to get anything off of his book."

Ben's last words to me echoed through my mind: "Pay it forward." This was my chance to "pay it forward" for my best friend and his wife. Somehow, someway I was going to make this right — for Ben.

"Well, you know what, Dan? I'm not going to let that happen," I said defiantly.

"I'm not the enemy here, Luke. My hands are tied. There's nothing I can do if he didn't sign the form. We always push the old guys to sign it, but young guys like you and Ben, we just don't push it that hard," Dan said. "I'm sorry."

In an instant, my anger turned to quiet confidence. Where it came from, I don't know. "I'm going to figure out a way. Ben gave his heart and soul to his clients and this firm. It's not right, and I'm not going to let it happen. I just need to know that you'll back me on this."

"If you can figure out a way — as long as it's legal and doesn't violate any firm policies, I'll go to bat for you, Luke. Deal?"

"All right," I replied. "Thanks for letting me know."

I turned and headed to the den. I realized I didn't have the slightest idea how I was going to get Cindy paid out from Ben's book. But I'd been at the firm long enough to know that there was always a way. It was just a question of finding the right person and getting them on your side.

An attorney wouldn't help because Ben hadn't signed the form, so we had no legal case. I hadn't signed one either. Signing my form would be priority number 1 on Monday morning. That much I did know.

When I finally made it to the den, I was happy to see it was mostly family there. Aimee was standing with Cindy and Ben's two sisters. I caught her eye and winked. Betty looked dazed, sitting on the couch with her little white dog in her lap. She was surrounded by Joe's sisters and a couple of her friends I recognized from the neighborhood.

Joe's face lit up as soon as he saw me. Ben's family had adopted me when my parents got divorced. I was an awkward 11-year-old, and my mom had to work all the time. When I started hanging out with Ben, Joe took me under his wing. I spent a lot of time at their house, and he always treated me like one of his own kids.

He used to take Ben and me down to the docks where he ran his shipping company. Sometimes he even pulled some strings so he could take us on the huge ships that carried freight cars full of stuff all over the world.

To me, being on the docks was like being in *Honey, I Shrunk the Kids*. Everything there was built to a larger-than-life scale, which fit Joe's personality perfectly. He was a gregarious, kindhearted man, always eager to make you smile or help you out. It was obvious where Ben got it from.

Ben and I spent summers working for Joe. He'd paid us well but expected as much out of us as he did any other employee, sometimes more. It was the hardest physical work I've ever done in my life, but we were buff by the end of every summer. I'm convinced that's how I made the high school football team.

"Luke. Good to see you," Joe boomed. I noticed immediately how tired he looked. The lines on his face ran deeper than usual, and his eyes drooped like a basset hound's. When he hugged me, I noticed he did so a little harder and a little longer than usual.

He shoved a beer in my hand and whispered in my ear, "There's someone I want you to meet. Let's go for a walk."

I followed him out the French doors to the pool. It was refreshing to get away from the crowded house and especially away from Dan. The cool, fresh air felt good, and I sucked it in eagerly.

Joe was a character. I'd describe him as flamboyant but very direct. What you see is what you get with Joe. I watched as he squinted in the darkness, obviously searching for someone.

"Follow me," he said.

Joe had piqued my curiosity. This cloak-and-dagger stuff

wasn't really his style. "So who exactly are you looking for, Joe?" I asked, somewhat amused.

"The smartest man I know," he answered quietly. "I've known him a long time, and he's a business genius. If it wasn't for him, I wouldn't even have my business. He helped me get it going back when I was young and stupid and didn't have a clue what I was doing. It was *his* smarts that took it from a random group of clients when and where I could get them, to operating like a real business. He systematized every important aspect and helped me get to the next level. He was my financial advisor for a while too and got me on the right track early."

"Wait, he was your financial advisor?" I guess it never dawned on me that someone handled Joe's money before Ben.

Joe nodded. "Taught me how to make a fortune in my business and then helped me make a fortune with my investments. When I decided to sell part of the business, I contacted him. He put together the deal, the transition plan for existing customers and found the buyers — everything. I owe a lot to him."

"Is he still a financial advisor?" I asked, wondering how one person could possibly do all that.

"Not anymore. He went into venture capital or something like that. I don't really know. From what I hear, now he just flies around the world doing deals."

I'd never heard Joe talk about anyone like this. He was not one to lavish praise on anybody much less give them credit for his business. He always prided himself on being completely self-made.

"Betty and I were just kids when we got married and Ben was on the way before we knew it..." He stared off into the distance, a faraway look in his eyes, like he'd been transported to a different time and place. He didn't say anything for a long time, and neither did I.

"Then I lost my job," Joe murmured. "To me it was the

end of the world. I was drinking in this bar down by the docks wondering how I was going to tell Betty. Then," he paused, "Victor just...appeared."

The way he said it struck me as odd. "What do you mean he just appeared?" I asked.

Ignoring my question, he continued, "Things—good things happen when Victor appears."

I was confused, and Joe was acting weird. *Probably the stress of losing Ben,* I thought.

Then he grabbed me by the shoulders. Tears were streaming down his face. "When you and Ben decided to be partners, I knew it was time," he choked.

"Time for what?" I asked as gently as I could.

"Time to contact Victor. It was time for him to do for you and your business what he did for me. Change it. Change you," he cried, desperate for me to understand.

"Now Ben's gone," he sobbed.

It was as if every emotion Joe had held in since Tuesday came pouring out all at once. I knew there was nothing I could say or do to make it better. So I just waited.

After several minutes, he tried to compose himself. He yanked a handkerchief from his pocket and wiped his eyes. "This was my gift. I wanted it for both of you, but now it's just you, Luke. Victor will help you systematize your business and Ben's. He'll see to it that you...you reach your potential." His voice trailed off. Then he whispered, "That's what he does."

I just stared at him. What the hell was he talking about?

I figured now was probably not the time to tell him that our partnership was null and void and that Cindy wasn't going to get a penny off of Ben's book. First the conversation with Dan, and now this. My head was spinning.

Joe pointed to the side street. A black Mercedes limo was just pulling up to the curb. "There he is. Good luck, son." And just like that, he turned and walked away.

I glanced at the Mercedes as it skillfully pulled into a spot that looked a size too small. Then I turned and watched Joe amble toward the house.

"Joe, wait," I called, but he just kept walking.

I stood there in disbelief as he paused, then disappeared into the house without me. What was this, the *Twilight Zone* or something? Eyeing the mysterious car again, I noticed the driver now standing at attention next to the passenger door. *What the hell,* I thought and slowly wandered over in that direction.

I tugged at the heavy wrought iron gate. It whined in protest as it swung open. The driver's greeting was warm but formal. "Good evening, Mr. Somers."

"Uh, good evening," I managed.

The driver looked to be in his late 60s, thin and meticulously dressed. "Mr. Guise is expecting you," he said cheerfully as he opened the door and motioned for me to get in the car.

I hesitated. Should I call Aimee and tell her? Tell her what I wondered — that I wasn't going to make Ben's celebration? Instead, I was getting in a strange car with a strange man I'd never met and wasn't sure when I'd be back. I decided to let Joe handle that. The driver waited patiently until I finally climbed in. The door immediately shut behind me.

"Hello, Luke. My name is Victor Guise."

I found myself sitting across from a distinguished-looking gentleman. He wore the most elegant suit I'd ever seen, and it was obvious he worked out regularly. Even with silver hair, he looked younger than Joe though I knew he couldn't be. The first thing I noticed was his eyes. They were pale blue, kind but intense at the same time. I felt self-conscious under his gaze and caught myself squirming in the luxurious leather seat.

"Please accept my condolences. I know you and Ben were very close."

"Thanks," I muttered. The car was moving now, and I

fought the urge to fling open the door and throw myself out.

"Can I interest you in a beer?" he asked with a smile that immediately put me at ease.

His offer surprised me. He didn't strike me as a beer drinker. I wondered if it would be Dos Equis, and he was actually the most interesting man in the world. I pushed the thought from my mind.

"Yes, sir," I replied, feeling the need to address him formally even though that wasn't usually my style. "That would be great."

He pulled two bottles out of the fridge along with two frosted goblets. He opened them, poured a rich coppery-colored liquid into one of the goblets, and handed it to me, along with the bottle.

I took a long sip of the beer. It took every ounce of willpower I had not to guzzle it. "This could be the best beer I've ever tasted!"

"I'm glad you like it. It's a Trappist beer. Chimay Grande Reserve from Belgium."

I had no idea what a Trappist beer was, but I made a mental note to Google it when I got home. I started to feel a calmness I hadn't felt since Ben's death. It could have been the beer, but somehow I knew it was the man I was with.

"Joe thinks very highly of you," I said. "In fact, I've never heard him talk about anybody the way he talked about you just now."

He smiled. "Joe is good man. I just hope he's able to recover from Ben's death. It concerns me greatly."

I nodded and felt the week's melancholy creep back in. Feeling my throat starting to close again, I decided it was best to just keep talking. "He said you were his financial advisor."

"For a time I was."

"He said you could help me take my business to another level, systems, reach my potential—something like that," I mumbled.

"What do you think?" he asked, studying me carefully. "About your potential, that is?"

I poured the rest of my beer in the oversized glass and considered his question. "Well, Ben and I both worked really hard to get to where we are...were...whatever," I said. "I know I'm not as efficient as I could be. Joe said you helped him build systems in his business, and that's when it really took off. Ben was good with systems..."

My vision started to blur as tears filled my eyes again. Sadness, stress, and extreme fatigue had finally caught up to me. I looked down, trying to hide it, but the teardrops just splattered in my lap.

Victor was silent and handed me a silk handkerchief with some kind of monogram on it—maybe an 8. There could have been a fly on it for all I cared. I just buried my eyes in it and wept.

"I'm sorry," I groaned, embarrassed. I couldn't believe I was crying in front of this man I'd just met.

"There's no need to apologize. I would question your character if you felt any differently," he said gently.

I tried to pull myself together and then blurted out, "I don't know what my potential is, but I know I'm not close to it, and to be honest, I don't know if I ever will be. I work hard, but I don't work very smart, and I'm sick of constantly reinventing the wheel for every client that walks through the door. I waste a lot of time and spend way too much of it trying to figure out what to do next. My client service is marginal because I never have time, so I don't get the referrals I need to grow like I want to. And I couldn't tell you the last time I actually did anything to get new clients. I used to dream of being a million-dollar producer, but I've been at this stupid plateau forever. Our partnership was supposed to be the spark I needed to move past it...but now that's gone too."

"Is that it?" he asked.

"I guess that about covers it," I sighed.

"Do you want to change?"

"Of course I want to change," I snapped, surprised by my own ferocity.

"I don't ask that facetiously," he said. I could feel his eyes boring right through me even though I was still staring at my lap. "Many people say they want to change, but you must recognize that everything has a price. Most people are not willing to pay that price in terms of the time, energy, and effort it takes to be truly successful.

"I suppose that's true," I agreed.

"Real success is measured not only financially, but also, in the lives you touch, the difference you make and what you give back. By becoming more 'efficient' as you say, you're not only able to raise your net worth, but more importantly, you're able to make a bigger difference in more lives. Would you agree?"

"Yes, sir," I answered earnestly. My mood started to lift. I believed in what he was saying.

"Now, do you want to change, Luke?"

"Yes, sir. I need to...for my clients, for the prospects I know I can help, for Ben and Joe, for my family, and for me."

He studied me for several seconds without saying a word. Then a smile slowly spread across his face. "Very well then. Are you familiar with the old Madison home at the top of the hill?"

"Yes, sir." I nodded.

"That's where I'll be staying. Please speak to Henry to coordinate the schedule. You will visit me once a week until the necessary changes have been completed."

I was relieved I hadn't blown it with Joe's friend. "Yes, sir. Thanks for the opportunity. You won't be sorry."

"I don't expect to be," he said calmly.

The car slowed to a stop, and I realized I had absolutely no idea where we were or how long we'd been driving. The door opened, and the driver, whom I assumed was Henry, stood waiting patiently. I climbed out of the huge car.

"And, Luke," Victor called.

"Yes, sir?"

"You must do *exactly* as I say. Do you understand?"

"Yes, sir."

Henry gently closed the door behind me. He handed me a card with only a phone number printed on it.

"Please contact me at this number on Monday morning, and I will advise you as to Mr. Guise's availability."

"Uh, okay. Thanks," I said tentatively.

"You are quite welcome, sir. Have a pleasant evening."

And with that, he eased back into the car and drove off. As the black car disappeared into the night, I looked around and realized I was standing at the end of Joe's driveway. The streets were empty now. The celebration of Ben was over.

Suddenly, I remembered Aimee. I hoped she wouldn't be too angry that I abandoned her for the evening. I hurried up the driveway. It had been a very strange evening, but I felt good—better than I had in a very long time. I could hardly wait until my first appointment with the mysterious Victor Guise.

2. GETTING ORGANIZED

"If you do not change direction, you may end up where you are heading."

— Lao Tzu

Thank God it was Thursday. Somehow I'd managed to fumble my way through the first three days of the week, which had been anything but easy. There was a dark and unmistakable void in the office next to mine, the office that, until last Tuesday, belonged to Ben.

I still remember how excited we were when we finally graduated from the bull pen to real offices. Ben and I had splurged on a bottle of Dom Perignon, which he secretly chilled in his office all afternoon. As soon as the place cleared out, we'd called Aimee and Cindy. They raided the local specialty store and arrived with a delectable spread of fancy French cheeses and hors d'oeuvres. We celebrated in Ben's office until every morsel of food and drop of champagne was gone.

That night, we felt invincible—like we ruled the world, and the new offices were our castle. Nothing could stop us...

or so we thought. Now when I passed his empty office, it took everything I had to avoid being sucked into a black hole of grief.

Dan barged into my office bright and early Monday morning and immediately started hounding me for the list of clients I knew from Ben's book. I'd glanced at the list, checked off a few names in addition to family, and shoved it back at him. He seemed satisfied and lumbered out of my office, a man on a mission.

It took a lot of coaxing, begging, and pleading, but I finally convinced Dan to postpone handing out Ben's accounts for a few days. I needed some time to figure out what I could do to get Cindy the income she deserved off of Ben's book. He promised to hold off as long as he could, but I knew he was in a tough spot. The other advisors were circling like sharks, waiting for the accounts to be distributed.

Other than that, it was business as usual around the office. But I wasn't ready for business as usual. At least not yet.

The first call I'd made on Monday morning was to Henry, and he'd scheduled our regular meetings for Thursdays. Today was the day I'd been waiting for all week. Today I was meeting with Victor Guise. As I stared out of the window, I thought about our first encounter in the limo.

He and Joe were so different. It was hard to believe they'd been such good friends for such a long time. Joe was successful, but blue-collar successful, and I admired him for it. Victor Guise, on the other hand, was successful, but sophisticated, powerful successful. The way Joe talked about him was so out of character, almost reverent.

I also wondered why, if he'd been that instrumental in the success of his business, Joe hadn't mentioned him before. Had Ben ever met him? Had he even known about him? If he had, why hadn't he mentioned him to me? I secretly wondered if Victor Guise was in the Mafia or something and that's why no one ever talked about him. He traveled around the world doing deals. That's what Joe had said. What exactly did that even mean? What kind of deals?

Intriguing — that's how I'd describe him. Victor certainly had the mystery thing going, and I couldn't help but be curious about the guy. Even in the brief time I was with him, I could tell he was a private man, but beneath his calm demeanor lay power. Yet he was warm at the same time. His affection and concern for Joe was genuine. When I broke down, which I still can't believe I did, he was kind and understanding — almost grandfatherly. Yep, Victor Guise was a paradox all right. I wondered if he could do for my business what he'd done for Joe's.

"Luke...Excuse me...Luke?"

Startled, I spun around in my chair to see Randy Thomas, the newest advisor in the office, standing in the doorway. The firm had come up with another one of their brilliant initiatives, where the established advisors were supposed to mentor younger ones. Randy was my charge. If he made his numbers, I got some kind of bonus for my time.

It sounded good in theory, but unfortunately in practice most established advisors couldn't be bothered, so most of the new guys were on their own. Back when Ben and I started in the business, the firm never fired anyone. They just waited for you to starve to death and quit. Now, they had to hit some pretty tough numbers, and if they didn't within the allotted period of time, they were out. Fired. Gone.

Randy was a good kid, so I did what I could to help him along. He was young, probably about 26, though he looked maybe 20. He had strawberry blond hair that always seemed to be hanging in his eyes and a spattering of freckles across his nose and cheeks. The combination didn't exactly work in his favor. No one in their 50s or 60s was going to turn over their life savings to a kid who looked like he'd just started shaving.

He was smart though, and a hard worker. He also

appeared to be an eternal optimist, sometimes to the point of annoyance. Once he'd hit his first asset and production goals, I'd given him most of my C and D accounts to work. He did well with them and actually managed to find additional money. Even though he was young, he was good with people. He had a comfortable, easygoing manner and was outstanding when it came to customer service. Most rookies didn't make it past the first six months, but he was well into his second year. There was a chance he just might make it.

"Hey, Randy, what can I help you with?" I asked.

He had a couple of warm prospects and wanted some advice on what his next steps should be with them. We went through each one, and I gave him my thoughts.

Ordinarily I wouldn't have much time to spend with him, but today was different. I wasn't really in the mood to get on the phone with anyone, and I had some time to burn before leaving for Victor's. He must have sensed that and took advantage of the extra attention.

"Hey, Luke, can I ask you something?" He had a habit of squinting and crinkling his nose when he was thinking, just like my son Ethan. It made him look even younger to me.

"Sure. What's on your mind?" I answered.

"Well, I was just wondering. How long were you in the business before you *knew* you were going to make it?"

Reading between the lines, I laughed. "You mean how long before I wasn't completely paranoid I *wasn't* going to make it?"

He grinned. "Yeah, I guess that's what I really meant."

I carefully considered his question, trying to remember exactly when I realized I just might have a shot of making it as an advisor. "I'd have to say it was when I had my first $10,000 month. Once I hit 10 grand in gross, I never went below it again."

He frowned. "Guess I have a ways to go," he sighed.

"It's different for everybody, Randy," I added quickly.

"That was just me. You may feel like you don't have to worry anymore when you hit some other point. Just keep going. Really, Randy, anything will work if you just work it hard and consistently. No matter what, don't doubt yourself and don't give up!"

"Okay, you know better than me. But I have to ask. Was there some real turning point where everything just came together for you?" he asked hopefully.

I smiled. "That's a long story, and I'd love to share it with you." I glanced at my watch and realized I should have left ten minutes ago.

Randy was very perceptive and noticed everything when he was with someone. He bounced out of his chair. "I'm ready whenever you are, but I know I've taken up a lot of your time. I hope we can talk again soon."

"Very soon," I promised as I shoved some last-minute items into my briefcase.

I had to admit I had a few butterflies as I made my way up the winding road to the old Madison home, as Victor had called it. The rest of us referred to it as the Madison mansion. It was at the top of the hill on the edge of town. I'd never been inside, but when Mr. Madison was still alive, he used to put on an amazing Christmas display every year. There were so many lights you could see them from the city.

I can remember as a kid, the whole hill seemed magical and twinkling at Christmastime. Everyone used to say that's how Santa found his way to us kids. He just looked for Madison Hill and followed his runway lights into the city.

Joe and Betty used to pile Ben, his sisters, me, and my mom, if she wasn't working, into their van. Betty would make hot chocolate and cookies, and we'd sing Christmas carols and munch on cookies all the way up the hill. Every year, Mr.

Madison would do something different with the lights and decorations, and we all couldn't wait to get up the hill to see it.

Good times, I mused. I hadn't been up there in years. In fact, I wasn't sure I'd even be able to find the turnoff without the Christmas traffic to signal I was getting close.

Mr. Madison died when Ben and I were seniors in high school. I remember because he used to buy our team flashy new football uniforms every year. We were always the best-dressed team on the field, and he never missed a game. It was a big deal when he died. We thought we were going to have to squeeze into the previous year's uniforms, but he had a ton of money, and the uniforms were taken care of in his will.

I eased off the gas as I searched for the turnoff. When I reached the top of the hill, it was obvious I'd missed it. I headed back down at a snail's pace, slowing to almost a stop at every potential opening in the heavy brush. Finally I spotted a road marked by an old mailbox that still read "Madison" in peeling red letters.

After about a quarter of a mile, the road opened up into a large parking area. I parked my car hastily, grabbed my briefcase, and bounded up the gravel path to the house. The old mansion was as magnificent as I remembered it. The wraparound porch was massive, as were the heavy, beveled glass doors that led inside.

I hesitated a moment and then rang the doorbell. Within seconds, Henry opened the door with a smile.

"Good afternoon, sir. It's very nice to see you again. Please come in," he said graciously.

"Thanks, Henry." I followed him into a stately marble foyer and marveled at the impressive crystal chandelier that loomed over the entrance. It looked more like a movie set than a place someone actually lived. "Wow," I gasped. "This place is amazing. Just like I imagined."

Henry smiled. "Right this way, sir. Mr. Guise is awaiting your arrival in the den."

He led me down a long, wide hallway lined with expensive-looking furniture, art, and lots of sculptures. The furniture was obviously Asian but simple rather than ornate.

"Are all these antiques?" I asked, admiring a pair of lion bookends.

"Yes. Most are from Thailand. Although, the bookends you're looking at are 19th-century Burmese roaring lions. Mr. Guise spends a great deal of time in Asia."

The mystery continues, I thought to myself.

"He's got a lot of different Buddha statues, but they all must watch their weight." I laughed, noticing the thin figures along the hall. "I always think of Buddha as a pretty chunky guy."

Henry stopped suddenly and turned serious. "The Fat Buddha or Laughing Buddha is an image exclusive to Chinese Buddhism. However, the Buddha taught and lived a life of moderation, so Mr. Guise feels it is disrespectful for people of any culture to portray him in a fat, gluttonous manner."

"Sorry. I—I didn't know. I didn't mean to be disrespectful," I stammered. "Is Mr. Guise Buddhist?"

Henry smiled again. "No, sir, he's not. However, he does have a great admiration for Buddhist teachings."

With that, Henry opened the door to the den. Still a little shaken from Henry's reaction to the Buddha thing, I walked rather tentatively into the enormous, but comfortable, room. One entire wall was floor-to-ceiling windows. The view was stunning—lush green rolling hills and a large deep-blue pond filled with Canadian geese.

Victor rose as soon as we entered and moved around his desk to shake my hand. He greeted me warmly. "Hello, Luke. How are you, my boy?"

"I'm doing well, thank you," I answered, feeling at ease again.

"Good! Have a seat over here where we can enjoy the view," he motioned in the general direction of two large leather chairs in front of the windows. "Henry, how about some of that exquisite strawberry lemonade of yours?"

"Right away, sir," he answered and quickly disappeared.

"So are you ready for this journey?" Victor had an unmistakable twinkle in his eye.

"Uh, yes, sir, I think so."

"Do you know why you're here?" Victor asked.

The truth was I had only a vague idea of why I was there, so I tried my best to formulate an answer that made sense. "Well, Joe said this was supposed to be his gift to Ben and me. But now," I hesitated, "there's only me. He said when you helped him build systems for his business, everything took off." I paused and then added, "He said you help people reach their potential. I guess that's what I really want."

He studied me for several seconds and then asked, "How motivated are you to change?"

"Very. I know I've grown complacent, and since Ben's gone, I'm afraid it's going to get worse. After 10 years in the business, I'm making a comfortable living, but I'm not growing."

"Why do you think that is?" he asked.

"I don't know," I muttered.

"Oh, I think you do," Victor challenged. "So I'm going to ask you again. Why do you think you're not growing?"

His tone had an edge to it. It surprised me how quickly he could go from grandfatherly to borderline confrontational.

Henry walked in with a pitcher and two glasses balanced on a sterling silver tray. He took his time pouring us each a glass of pinkish liquid. I was grateful for the time to think. I guess if this whole Victor thing was going to work for me like it did for Joe, I was going to have to be honest.

"Thank you, Henry," he said politely. Victor took a long sip and called to Henry as he was leaving, "Exceptional as usual."

"Thank you, sir." Henry smiled, obviously pleased. He

gently closed the door behind him, and the two of us were alone again.

He turned to me and resumed. "Now, you were saying?"

"Well, I guess I've spent so many years working in my practice, I've gotten tired and satisfied with where I am. I never make the time to work on my practice. I know I'm just winging it, and actually, I'm lucky to have the numbers I do, but...I don't want my luck to run out. My partnership with Ben was going to be the spark I needed to start working on my business and growing again," I said honestly. "I know I'm capable of a lot more than I'm doing. It's time I started running my practice like a real business."

"That's more like it," he said, smiling. "I have two rules, my boy. First, you must be willing to be perfectly honest with me in all respects—your thoughts, your feelings, and exactly what's happening or not happening in your business. That's essential if I'm going to help you. Secondly, as I mentioned in the car, you must do *exactly* as I instruct you to do. Are these conditions acceptable to you?"

"Yes, sir, they are."

"Then let's get started, shall we?"

"Yes, sir," I said enthusiastically as I pulled out a new notebook and my special "Victor" pen. I have a bit of a pen fetish. I knew meetings with this man were going to be special, and that called for a new pen. I'd chosen a beauty too—silver, slim, and sophisticated. It reminded me of Victor.

I settled into my leather chair. "I'm ready," I announced.

Victor took another long sip from his glass. "We simply cannot proceed until you try Henry's strawberry lemonade. It's like nectar from the gods."

I followed his lead and took a long sip of what might have been the most perfect nonalcoholic beverage I'd ever tasted. In fact, a shot of vodka and it would be perfection in the alcoholic category as well. "You're absolutely right! Nectar of the gods," I agreed.

There was a long silence as we both savored Henry's god nectar and took in the tranquil view outside. I was completely relaxed, watching the geese entertain themselves in the pond outside.

"It's important you understand, Luke, that what I'll be instructing you to do over the next few months is not magic, nor is it rocket science. What we will be doing together is creating clearly defined, repeatable systems for your business. These will increase your effectiveness by giving you structure in how you operate on a daily basis. If you follow my instructions, both you and your clients will be happier; you'll feel confident and in control; and your referrals, assets, and revenue will all increase. You will be doing what successful people do and what average people won't. However, don't be fooled by the simplicity of some of the instructions I give you. As you complete these tasks, you will move closer to your potential, and that is my hope for you. Do you understand?"

"Yes, sir. I understand."

"Very well then. Today, we're going to begin with the basics and address your organization and time management. It's an essential piece of your success puzzle, but first, tell me. What do you do when you wake up in the morning?" Victor asked quietly.

Honesty – he made me promise, I reminded myself. "I usually have a cup of coffee, get in the shower, and get dressed. I try to have breakfast with the family, but usually I'm running late, so I grab something to eat on my way out the door and head to the office."

"And would you consider that an appropriate success ritual?"

"Well, I'm not really sure what a success ritual is, but I'm pretty sure it's not that," I answered.

He laughed. "And you'd be right, my boy. You must begin to program your mind for success from the moment you wake up in the morning. It sets the tone for your entire day."

I wrote in big letters across the top of my page, "Morning Success Ritual." I continued to write as fast as I could as Victor spoke.

"A success ritual is a very personal thing, and you must begin your day with one that works for you. Just like many things we'll discuss over the next several months, consistency is of utmost importance. If you find yourself always running late, I'd like to suggest a novel idea."

"What's that?" I asked.

"I would suggest you wake up an hour earlier." He smiled.

"I really set myself up for that one, didn't I?"

"Indeed you did. What kind of day can you expect when you're rushing out the door with a bagel in your mouth?"

"I guess that's true." I laughed. "But an hour earlier?"

"Exactly as I say, remember?"

"Okay, an hour earlier," I conceded. "So what do I do with that hour?"

"You must determine that for yourself, but let me give you an example. I wake up and immediately drink a glass of water that I keep at my bedside. After six to eight hours of sleep with nothing to drink, my body is dehydrated. So first, I take care of my body. Then I engage my mind in silence."

"You mean like meditation?" I felt compelled to share with him my dismal track record with meditation. "Every time I've tried to meditate, my mind is all over the place. Everybody says it works so great, but I've never noticed any difference at all."

"It can be meditation or prayer or just enjoying the quiet before your day begins. It's all about what works for you. And for the record, when I first started, my mind wandered as well. It's not so much what you do or even how effective it is in the beginning. It's about developing the habit of giving your mind some calm, relaxing time before you start your day."

I wrote "Silence" in my notebook. I was skeptical, but I promised to try it.

Victor continued, "Another thing I do is write down my most critical goals for the day. These are the things that I absolutely, unequivocally commit to accomplishing that day. Writing them down gives me clarity."

"You mean like a to-do list?"

"Not exactly," he answered. A to-do list is much more detailed and more about the 'how' of your day. We'll talk about that later. What I'm talking about here is more big-picture goals for the day — the 'what' of your day, if you will."

I scribbled "Goals" in my notebook. Whatever Victor was doing obviously worked for him. I was hoping this "success ritual" thing would work for me too.

"Next, I spend some time on visualization. It is widely acknowledged by professional athletes, actors, and other successful people as a critical tool for their success. As I'm sure you know, many studies have been done on the power of visualization."

"Yeah, I remember reading about some study with basketball players practicing free throws. As I recall, the group that just visualized free throws did almost as well as the group that actually practiced them."

"The important thing to remember about visualization is that you must use as many of your senses as possible to imagine the results you seek. It's not enough to just see it. You must feel it, hear it, and touch it as well. In other words, visualize in HD."

"I've tried visualization before, but I just visualized it. You know — tried to see it. I never tried to feel it or use any other senses at all. I can see how that would make it more powerful. So what else goes into a success ritual?"

I was starting to get excited. It was clear that starting my day with a success ritual instead of with my usual hectic rushing-out-the-door habit could make a difference in how the rest of the day went. Aimee was going to freak out when I told her I was going to start waking up an hour earlier. She was a morning person and always up before the sun, whereas I'd always been a big fan of the Snooze button.

Victor continued, "I also make it a point to read something positive or inspirational every morning, even if it's only for fifteen minutes. It's something I've done since I was very young, and I enjoy it."

"Like a self-help thing?"

"Sometimes. And sometimes it's a biography or memoir of someone I find interesting or inspiring."

"Hmm. I always hear these great quotes by Henry Ford. Maybe I'll start with him," I said.

"Start with whomever you like. The only thing that matters is that you are inspired. The final component of my success ritual is exercise. You must get your blood pumping early in the day."

"We...I mean, I go to the gym every day after work. Does that count as part of my morning success ritual?"

"No doubt your time at the gym is invaluable to your success. It builds confidence while improving your health. So by all means, continue. However, in the morning I'm talking about just five minutes of some sort of exercise that will get the blood flowing. It can be push-ups, sit-ups, yoga — whatever you feel will best contribute to your daily success and get you moving."

"That makes sense. I can do anything for five minutes," I declared. "Even in the morning."

"Keep in mind, Luke, that this is *my* success ritual. Yours may be completely different. Give careful consideration to what activities would contribute the most to your daily success and in programming your mind to believe in your success."

I gulped down the rest of my lemonade. Already, I felt more empowered. Could it be I was actually looking forward to waking up an hour earlier tomorrow? My life was already starting to change!

"Now let's talk about your day once you get to the office," Victor continued.

"Like I said in the car, I know I waste a lot of time during the day."

"That leads me to the obvious question. Do you create a prioritized to-do list before you leave the office each day?"

"Sometimes," I answered and then remembered my pledge of honesty. "But not really."

Undeterred by my answer, he continued, "Your to-do list should not just consist of simple items to check off one by one. You should look at it as a critical tool in your business arsenal. In order for that to happen, you have to follow certain to-do list rules. The first of which is to prepare it before you leave the office at the end of the day. Do you know why?"

"I would guess so it's already done when you walk in the door and you don't have to waste any time trying to figure out what to do first."

"That's a big part of it. A lot of advisors think they can do an effective to-do list in the morning. Perhaps that may work at times, but more often than not, it won't.

"Think about it. You come in fully intending to do your to-do list before you do anything else. The markets drop dramatically, you have frantic clients calling, and then your assistant calls in sick. What are the chances you'll get around to that to-do list now?"

"Not very good." I recalled how many days I had that began just like that.

He nodded and continued, "Now it's midmorning, and the day finally begins to calm down. If you do a to-do list at all, odds are it will be haphazard at best. The more probable outcome is that you 'wing it,' as you say, and don't do one at all. Would you agree?"

"You're right. You must have a hidden camera in my office!"

Victor chuckled. "No need. Not only have I seen it, but in my younger years, I lived it."

Somehow I just couldn't picture Victor without a detailed to-do list in front of him at all times. I laughed at the thought. "Glad I'm not unique."

"Another reason to formulate your to-do list the night before is because it gives you the opportunity to approach it more analytically. You have some distance, so you write down what actually needs to be done rather than what you feel like doing at the time."

"I see your point there," I said as I made some notes in my notebook.

"Are you familiar with the 80/20 rule?" Victor asked abruptly.

"Sure. Eighty percent of your business comes from 20% of your clients."

"It's true of more than just your revenue. It's also true when it comes to your to-do list. Eighty percent of your results are going to come from 20% of your tasks. However, human nature being what it is, we tend to focus on the 80% first, to 'get it out the way' so we can clear time to focus on the results-oriented 20%. A time that often never comes."

"I've never thought of it like that before, but you're right," I agreed. "And the 20% always seems to be the hardest stuff too — the stuff you don't want to do and always put off."

"That's precisely why you must prioritize your to-do list. You prioritize it so that you're focusing on those results-oriented tasks first."

"Prioritize it how exactly?"

"Ah, another rule of the to-do list," he answered. "A tasks are tasks that *must* be done. They tend to be appointments and phone calls. Plan on no more than three A tasks per day on your list. This will set you up for success in completing them. A tasks are the tasks that produce the most results. Would you agree?"

I nodded.

"B tasks are those that *should* be done. These are things like research, proposals, meeting prep. Some of your B tasks can and should be delegated — like meeting prep, for instance. C tasks are tasks that would be nice to get done but aren't critical to your success."

"You mean like organize your desk or read the *Wall Street Journal*?"

"Exactly. You must do your A tasks first. You cannot move on to B tasks until your A tasks are completed, and you can't move on to C tasks until your B tasks are completed. The only exception to this rule is if you're waiting on a return call from someone. Do you understand?"

"Got it!"

"I might also add that 'Call Clients' is not a legitimate A task. It's too vague. However, 'Call Clients' with a listing of the clients you wish to call and a brief note about what you plan to talk with them about *is* a legitimate A task."

"So the key is to be detailed with your to-do list," I observed.

"The more detailed it is, the more effective it is, and the more effective it is, the more of a real tool it is in your business. I would also suggest that you have your calendar in front of you as you work on your to-do list. Have at least a general idea of when you plan to do what tasks. Also, number the items on your to-do list in the order you plan to do them. Should you get distracted at any point during the day, the numbering allows you to get back on task much quicker with little or no internal debate."

"That's going to take a lot more time than I'm used to putting into a to-do list — when I do one at all."

"In the beginning, that may be true, but you will find after a week or so of devoting the necessary time to your to-do list, it will become much less time-consuming. And that brings me to my next point — time blocking. Do you do it?"

"No. I know it works. Ben used to do it a lot, but like I said before, over the last few years, I've been mostly winging it."

"Your winging it stops today," he said sternly. "Do you understand?"

"Yes, sir."

"Like the to-do list, time-blocking will add structure to your day and increase your effectiveness exponentially. Start your time-blocking process off slowly and then build upon it. By that I mean start with two 30- to 45-minute blocks. One in the morning and one in the afternoon. What do you feel are the most important tasks for you to begin blocking?"

"Well, I know I need to block out time to do the to-do list. That's a given. That would be the afternoon block. And it would be great to get all my calls out of the way first thing in the morning, so I'd say I'd reserve my morning block for that."

"Excellent! Now you must think of your time blocks as appointments with yourself and treat them accordingly — just as you would any other appointment. That means your door should be closed. Your phone should be on 'Do Not Disturb,' and you must make it very clear to your assistant that you are not to be disturbed unless there's an emergency or a market-sensitive call that comes in. Do you think you can do that?"

"I can try," I answered.

"Try is no longer acceptable, my boy. I believe it was Yoda who said, 'Try not. Do...or do not. There is no try.' Am I right?"

"Right are you." I laughed, impressed that a man Victor's age could or would quote Yoda. There was a lot that surprised me about this man.

"I would suggest you integrate your time blocks into your to-do list as a task until they become a habit. Schedule them at predetermined times, preferably at the same time every day."

"So what if I want or need to increase the time in each block? Is that okay to do?"

"Do not increase the length of your time blocks until you've completed your two 30-minute blocks every day for five consecutive days. Then increase them in 15-minute increments. Your time blocks should never exceed 60 minutes."

"Why not?" I asked.

"I want you to be in the habit of always setting yourself up for success. The probability of you adhering to a time block of over 60 minutes long-term is low. We want to establish habits you can adhere to regardless of what is happening around you. Do you understand?"

"Yes, sir, but what about adding more time blocks?"

"Only add an additional time block when you have successfully used your time blocks every day for an entire production month. And when you add one, have a good reason for doing so. Time blocks are a commitment."

"Sheesh. It's been a long time since I've had this much structure to my day. I hope I have the discipline to do all this," I said as my enthusiasm faded into the reality of what he was asking me to do.

"Discipline in any area of your life is a peculiar thing, Luke. More often than not, it is what we avoid and fight the most, yet when we have it, we are the happiest and feel the most powerful and in control. Remember that, my boy, and you will do well. Very well."

"Thank you, sir."

"The pleasure is mine, Luke." He stretched, stood up, and calmly scanned the scenery outside the window.

After one visit with Victor, I already knew Joe was right. I felt myself starting to believe again—that maybe my business *could* go to a whole new level, and maybe, just maybe, I could become a million-dollar producer. After all, that's what I'd dreamed of since I'd been in the business. I was determined to adhere to his two simple rules — be honest and do *exactly* as he said. I could do that. I wanted to do that.

I tossed my notebook and pen into my briefcase and suddenly thought of Cindy. If anyone could give me direction on the seemingly impossible situation with Cindy and Ben's book, it was Victor.

"Excuse me, sir," I said.

He turned to face me.

"Uh, I could use your advice on something."

"Certainly, my boy. What can I help you with?"

"It's about Cindy, Ben's wife...I mean, widow." Those words sounded so foreign to me. My mind still resisted, but I continued, "When an advisor dies, the surviving spouse is eligible to receive income off of the advisor's book for five years, but only if they sign this form."

"And let me guess," he said. "Ben didn't sign the FFASA form."

I was shocked he knew the actual name of the form. I didn't even remember it.

"No, sir, he didn't," I replied. "My manager says there's nothing anybody can do — firm policy and all that. But I've been around long enough to know that there's always a way if you can get to the right person. I *have* to make this right, but I don't know where to begin. I was hoping maybe you could give some direction."

His expression changed, hardened. It was like he transformed into a different person right before my eyes. To be honest, it kind of freaked me out. I wondered if I should have brought it up at all.

"Have the accounts been distributed yet?" he asked intensely.

"Uh no, not yet. I talked my manager into waiting until Monday."

"Good," he snapped. "How many advisors are in your office?"

"Twenty-seven," I answered.

"Are they all eligible in the production ranking for account distribution?"

His knowledge of the business amazed me. I knew he'd been an advisor, but that was a long time ago. How could he possibly know all the constantly changing rules and policies in place now?

"All but a few — the rookies and a couple of guys who never take accounts when an advisor leaves...or I guess dies."

"Listen carefully, Luke. Tomorrow, find out what the standard sliding scale is for a deceased sunset agreement. You must get every advisor who will get accounts to agree to the sliding scale and sign a joint account agreement. Understood?"

"Yes, sir," I answered. "Is that it?"

"Once you have all the signed agreements, deliver them to your manager. What's his name, and what's your branch number?"

"Dan Chapman and the branch is 360," I replied.

Victor snatched a pad from his desk and scribbled down the information. Then he looked up, his ice-blue eyes blazing. "Call Henry when it's done."

CHAPTER TO-DO LIST

1. Develop your own Morning Success Ritual. Do what you know will work best in preparing you for a successful day. Some suggestions are as follows:

    *   Meditation

    *   Writing down the day's big-picture goals — the "what" of your day

    *   Visualization — use as many senses as possible to make it real

    *   Exercise — not intended to be your full exercise program but rather something to get you moving and your blood pumping for the day

2. To-do List Rules

    *   Your to-do list must be done before you leave the office for the next day. Establish a time block for it in the afternoon.

    *   Prioritize it. Remember the 80/20 rule applies to your tasks as well as your revenue.

        ➤ A tasks must be done — phone calls and appointments

        ➤ B tasks should be done and delegated whenever possible — research, proposals, market prep

        ➤ C tasks would be nice if they got done — cleaning off desk, reading *WSJ*

> ➤ You cannot move on to B tasks until A tasks are completed, and you cannot move on to C tasks until B tasks are completed. The only exception is if you're waiting on a call back from someone.

> ➤ Call Clients is not a legitimate A task. An example of a legitimate A task is Call Clients with a list of clients to be called and a brief note as to what you will talk to each one about.

3. Begin your time blocking with a 30- to 45-minute block in the morning for calling and one in the afternoon for your prioritized to-do list.

   • Time blocks are appointments with yourself and should be treated accordingly—schedule around them whenever possible, door should be closed, phone should be on Do Not Disturb, alert your assistant that you are not to be disturbed except for emergencies or market-sensitive calls.

   • Add to your time block in 15-minute increments and only after you have consistently adhered to your AM and PM time block for five consecutive days.

   • Only add an additional time block after you have adhered to your existing time blocks consistently for one full production month.

   • Time blocks are a commitment, so only add additional ones when you have a good reason for doing so.

- Integrate your time blocks into your to-do list until they are a habit.

- No time blocks should be over 60 minutes in length—the chances of you adhering long term to a time block of over 60 minutes are slim.

4. Remember your to-do list and your time blocking add structure to how you operate on a daily basis. Together, they will add to your effectiveness exponentially and therefore have the potential to increase your referrals, assets, and revenue.

For Additional Resources, go to:

www.executivetransformations.com/ plateau2pinnacle-additionalresources

3. PREPARE TO LEVERAGE

*"Miracles happen every day; change your
perception of what a miracle is and you'll see
them all around you."*

— Jon Bon Jovi

I'd groaned when the alarm went off an hour earlier.
Fortunately, I'd outlined everything I wanted to include in
my success ritual the night before, so once I was awake, it
went smoothly. I had a breakfast with Aimee and the kids and
felt energized not having to rush. I had to admit it was nice
starting my day ahead of schedule instead of behind.

I got to the office early the next day to begin my campaign
for Cindy. I followed Victor's instructions to the letter. First,
I researched the five-year split on a widow arrangement and
then printed out a stack of joint account agreements. Ben
was well liked around the office, but when it came to signing
away money, I had no idea what to expect from my lobbying
effort.

As it turned out, almost everyone was eager to help
and signed the joint account agreement without hesitation.

A couple of guys initially resisted, but they eventually succumbed to peer pressure from the rest of the office. It was all done and delivered to Dan before noon.

Dan was skeptical and tried to manage my expectations. "I'll do what I can," he said. "But don't expect any miracles because Ben didn't sign the agreement."

I told Dan I understood, but he didn't know I had Victor on my side. According to Joe, Victor's influence knew no boundaries. I wasn't so sure in this case, but I followed his instructions. I went straight from Dan's office to call Henry and told him it was done.

Then the waiting began. It was Friday, so I knew the process wouldn't even begin until Monday, and there was no telling how many layers of management the approval would have to work its way through. The corporate wheels moved very slowly at a large firm. I didn't expect to hear anything back at all for weeks, maybe months.

The weekend was family time, and that included Ben's family now. Aimee and I had picked up the twins, Zach and Zoe, and took all the kids to the zoo on Saturday. Then the girls went shopping while the boys and I had disappeared into the man cave to watch some college football. Cindy joined us later for dinner, and we tried our best to adjust to life without Ben.

I'd continued my success ritual through the weekend, and by Sunday morning, I hardly noticed my hour-earlier wake-up time. My mind still wandered whenever I tried to meditate, but I noticed a definite change in my attitude after just three days of my new habit. Aimee noticed it too and couldn't believe I'd kept it up through the weekend.

On Sunday night, I was diligent in planning my week. I'd spent 45 minutes writing out a detailed and prioritized to-do list for Monday. I'd incorporated my time blocks and numbered my tasks just as Victor had instructed.

When I left the house on Monday morning, I felt

proactive and prepared for the week ahead. But I wasn't prepared when Dan barged into my office on Monday afternoon. He flopped down in a chair in front of my desk, tapping his fingers impatiently. I was on the phone with one of my long-winded clients but somehow managed to cut the call short.

"What did you do?" he demanded.

I stared back at him, confused. "Uh, what exactly are we talking about here?"

"The whole Cindy thing." He was obviously as puzzled as I was. "I just got a call from the region. It's approved. She's going to get the five-year revenue deal effective immediately. And they said the decision came directly from the top. So how did you manage to do it, Luke?"

I grinned from ear to ear. *Victor,* I thought. How did he do it—that was the question!

"Just rallied the branch behind it and got the joint account agreements signed," I answered innocently.

"That's all you're going to tell me?"

"That's all I can tell you." I smiled.

He started to walk out of my office but turned and shook my hand. "I still don't know how you swung it, but good job, Luke."

I couldn't believe it. Victor had allowed me to keep my promise to Ben. Despite my joy, tears welled up in my eyes as the weight of what had just happened settled in. "This one's for you, buddy," I said quietly, hoping that, wherever he was, Ben could hear me.

I sat in the den waiting impatiently for Victor to enter the room. After several minutes, he strolled in from the side door.

"Sorry to keep you waiting, my boy." He smiled. "How was your week?"

"My week was great, thank you," I answered politely and then asked as calmly as I could, "How did you do it, sir?"

He gazed at me for several seconds, obviously amused. Finally he replied, "I assume you're referring to the unfortunate misunderstanding over Ben's book?"

"Yes, sir. That's exactly what I'm referring to!"

"I just went to the right person, Luke—as *you* astutely advised."

His generosity astounded me, but I knew that would be the extent of his explanation. I'd never know how he did it. I was just grateful he had. "Thank you, sir. You…you have no idea what this means to me."

Joe was right about Victor. Things…good things happen when he appears.

"The privilege was mine. Now, are you ready to get started?" he asked.

"Yes, sir," I said as I retrieved the notebook and special pen from my briefcase.

"Today, we're going to talk about leveraging your existing book."

"That's good because I don't really want to prospect anymore."

"I'm sure you don't. I take it you're familiar with the 'know your client' rule?"

"Sure. They start that conditioning on the Series 7!"

He nodded knowingly. "Then allow me to pose a question: how well do you think you 'know your book'?"

"I know it pretty well," I answered confidently. I couldn't be sure, but I had the distinct feeling I was being set up with this line of questioning.

The look of amusement returned to his face as he continued, "Effectively leveraging your book begins with knowing precisely who's who in your book and then implementing a superior client service model based on that knowledge.

"When was the last time you segmented your book? And I'm not talking about the typical book segmentation based on assets and revenue only. I'm talking about a comprehensive book segmentation that considers not only assets and revenue but also the important intangibles essential to really knowing your book."

I wasn't sure what he meant by "important intangibles," but I assumed I'd find out soon enough. "Well, it's been a while, but like I said, I know my book."

"Do you now?" he asked. "Then I'm sure you can tell me exactly how many A clients you have. And precisely how many of them have given you referrals in the past? And oh, by the way, do you have a B+ tier in your book for clients who could potentially become As? What about advocates? How many of those do you have in your book?"

"Well, I can't tell you all that right off the top of my head! But I know who my A clients are."

"Ah." He nodded. "Then you really don't know your book now, do you?"

He had me there. "Okay, so maybe I don't know it quite as well as I thought," I conceded. "But what kind of intangibles are you talking about?"

"Well, I've already touched on two. Who are your referral sources, and who are your advocates?"

"Aren't they the same thing?"

"Not necessarily. An advocate can definitely be someone who gives you referrals. However, it can also be someone who doesn't but rather talks you and your virtues up at every opportunity," he explained.

"I get it. I have a lady just like that. She's never actually given me a referral, but she told everybody in her book club about me. She even invited me to speak at one of their meetings. I've actually gotten a couple of really good accounts from that book club."

"That is an advocate," he acknowledged. "Other

intangibles you should consider are: Do you enjoy working with them? Do they take your advice? Do they have a potentially lucrative sphere of influence? What is their future revenue potential, and are they in some sort of recurring revenue platform?"

"I can see how that kind of information could be pretty valuable as part of a book segmentation."

"Indeed. These are all factors you should consider if you want your book segmentation to be a real tool in your business."

"That makes sense. I know how to do a regular book segmentation. But how do you do one like you're talking about?"

He cocked his head to one side as if suddenly deep in thought. "You know, I believe I'm ready for some of Henry's strawberry lemonade. What about you, my boy?"

"Uh, sure. Bring on the god nectar!"

He laughed. "God nectar it is!" He pressed the intercom button on his phone.

"Yes, sir?" Henry answered promptly.

He winked at me and spoke in his usual all-business tone. "Henry, we need two glasses of god nectar, please."

There was silence and then, "I beg your pardon, sir?"

"God nectar! Your celestial strawberry lemonade!"

"Ah, yes, sir," he said. "Right away, sir."

"Thank you, Henry," Victor said as he disconnected. "Now where were we? Ah yes—segmenting your book. I suggest you segment into A, B+, B, C, and D clients. The B+ tier is a very important one."

There was a soft knock on the door, and Henry entered with two crystal glasses perched on his silver tray.

"Excuse me, sir. Uh, 'god nectar' is served." He smiled.

"Thank you, Henry," said Victor. "That is a new term coined by our quite perceptive protégé here. One I believe is highly appropriate."

Henry nodded. "Thank you, sir. And thank you as well, Mr. Somers."

"You're welcome, Henry," I said. "It's great stuff!"

"Anything else, sir?" he asked, turning to Victor.

"All is well, Henry."

With that, Henry left us to our lemonade and book segmentation. There was a comfortable familiarity between Victor and Henry. I was sure Henry had worked for him for many years. It was obvious the two shared a genuine affection and respect for each other.

Victor sipped his lemonade as if he were savoring a fine wine for the first time. I, on the other hand, gulped mine down in seconds.

"So the B+ tier," I said. "That would be clients who aren't really As but aren't really Bs either?"

"Exactly," said Victor. "They are better than a typical B yet usually get grouped with the rest of the B clients. However, with a higher level of service and attention, they have the potential of being cultivated into A clients. Once this group is separated into a tier of its own, they often represent a 'sweet spot' within a book."

I couldn't believe how comprehensive Victor's book segmentation process was. It made me realize how important a process it really was when done right. "So what would be the breakpoint between an A and a B+?"

"Well, that depends on you and the nature of your book," Victor explained. "The assets and revenue breakpoints can be adjusted upward or downward depending on the nature of your book. Henry will have a packet for you at the end of our meeting today. In it will be a Quick and Easy Book Segmentation Point System© for incorporating all these factors into your segmentation process."

"That would be awesome! But how do you actually do it?"

"It's all in a spreadsheet." He pulled a piece of paper out

of one of his drawers and slid it toward me across the massive desk. "This is a sample of what it might look like."

I studied the sheet before me. It had four sections outlined in bold.

Book Segmentation:

Assets Points Assigned
$1 Million and Above = 4
$500,000–$999,999 = 3
$100,000–$499,999 = 2
< $100,000 = 1

Annual Revenue Points Assigned
$10,000 and Above = 4
$5,000–$9999 = 3
$1,000–$4,999 = 2
< $1,000 = 1

Intangibles Points Assigned
Enjoys working with them = 1/0
Takes your advice = 1/0
Gives referrals or advocate = 1/0
Sphere of influence potential = 1/0
Future revenue potential = 2/1/0
On recurring revenue platform = 1/0

Client Tier Points Earned
A Client = 12–15
B+ Client = 9–11
B Client = 7–8
C Client = 4–6
D Client = 2–3

He gave me some time to study the sheet before he continued, "Regardless of where you set your assets and revenue breakpoints, it's important to maintain the same number of breakpoints, and the same number of points per breakpoint for the tiers to work out the way they are here. Is that clear?"

"Yes, sir, I think so."

"You'll assign client points accordingly. Then add up the points for each client and place them in the appropriate client tier – A, B+, B, C, or D."

"What about the future revenue potential points? There are three choices there instead of just two like the other intangibles."

"That's completely up to you and is based purely on the nature of your own book," Victor explained. "One advisor may give 2 points to future revenue potential of $2 million, whereas another advisor may give 2 points to $500,000. This is another example of how the segmentation process can be tailored to fit your individual book. The three-point scale allows you to assign more points to those with a higher revenue potential while still giving one point to those with lesser, but solid potential."

I had to admit, I didn't know where to begin. "So what's the best way to work through the spreadsheet?"

"Begin by doing the quantitative analysis of your book and segment by assets and revenue. Assign points based on your breakpoints. Once you've completed that, evaluate each client according to the intangibles we've laid out on the spreadsheet and assign points accordingly. The spreadsheet will automatically calculate a point total for you. The points each client earns determines their client tier."

That made sense. I carefully considered the entire process. "I bet I'll have some surprises when I do this kind of segmentation."

"You'll discover that once you take the intangibles into consideration, some clients you thought were As will drop down to the B category and vice versa. I'd also recommend doing an ROA analysis by tier," he added.

"Why?" I asked. "You know the old 80/20 rule. The As are always the clients who pay the bills!"

"In most cases that is true," Victor agreed. "But not always. I recall one advisor who discovered that his revenue on a dollar basis was nearly even between his A and B+ tiers. However, the ROA on his B+ tier was nearly double that of his A tier due to the heavy discounting he did for A clients. Never underestimate the power of your B+ tier," he warned. "It may turn out to be that 'sweet spot' I mentioned."

"What about the bottom tier? I've inherited a lot of clients over the years. Even though I've given a lot of them to one of the junior advisors, I bet I still have a ton of accounts that end up as Cs or Ds."

"Ah, the great bottom-of-the-book debate." He smiled. "I would suggest you do the ROA analysis on those tiers as well. When you actually see the ROA on C and D accounts, it may be the catalyst you need to begin streamlining the bottom of your book. If you can't wrap it, purge it!"

I always felt a little guilty getting rid of C and D clients. So other than giving a few to Randy, I usually didn't. After all, those were the guys I built my business on.

As if reading my mind, Victor added, "You must consider time the currency of your business, my boy. The lower end of your book consumes valuable time for very little money and in many cases no money at all. You must begin spending your time wisely, and that means devoting it to the clients who pay you, appreciate you, and take your advice."

"I know you're right," I said reluctantly. "But do I need to get rid of them all?"

"That's a decision only you can make," he answered. "But there's also the liability factor to consider. These clients have experienced the same volatility and frustrations as everyone else in your book, but they probably don't receive a high level of service from you, do they?"

"Virtually none," I admitted. "I guess I could do a joint

number with this young guy in the office. That way if they ever win the lottery or something, I'll still get some benefit from holding on to them all these years."

"That's a possibility, but does that really eliminate your liability, or does it in fact increase it?"

"What do you mean?" I asked.

"If you choose to give accounts to a junior advisor and do it under a split number, yes, you share in whatever revenue may be generated. However, your name still appears on the statement. Therefore, the first problem you have is training these clients to call the junior advisor instead of you. Would you agree?"

"I guess so," I conceded. "But does that really increase my liability?"

"Think about it, Luke. You have a junior advisor making all of the decisions and recommendations, which means you have little or no control over what's happening in the account, yet your name is still on the statement. Who do you think the client will pursue if they ever consider legal action for any reason?"

"Both of us." I was starting to see his point about liability.

"It would be wise to weigh future revenue potential against your potential liability and then make the decision."

"Well, not everybody can go to the call center," I argued.

"That's true. However, another option is to *give* those accounts to a junior advisor. You may lose some revenue, but you carry no liability going forward. If the account had decent revenue potential, chances are it wouldn't be in the lower end of your book now, would it?"

I shrugged. I knew I wasn't going to win this debate.

Victor continued, "Occasionally, one of those accounts may inherit money or, as you mentioned, win the lottery, but those situations, as I'm sure you'll agree, are rare. It's time you made a decision on those clients once and for all, don't you think?"

"The inherited clients that I don't really know are one thing," I confessed. "But a lot of the accounts that seem small now are the ones that helped me get started in the beginning. I guess I feel bad getting rid of them."

"I understand that," he said gently. "Purging the lower end of the book can be a difficult process for advisors. However, with the ever-increasing fee structure at most firms, many of the lower-end clients are being charged a small fortune for little to no service in return. Sounds like a recipe for disaster to me."

"I know you're right. I don't know why it's so hard," I sighed.

"Might I suggest you use my Last Chance Letter to put them on notice that change could be coming?"

"What's that?" I asked, hopeful that somehow his letter might make it easier.

"It's a letter I wrote when I was experiencing the very same dilemma. The letter thanks your clients for their business over the years, informs them of the current fee structure, outlines their options, and offers them a final opportunity to move out of the lower end of the book by consolidating their assets."

I felt my face brighten. "That sounds good. At least I wouldn't be popping it on them."

"Excellent. Look for it in your packet."

"Okay, so I segment my book and get a clear idea of who's who in each tier. I get rid of some of the lower end of my book to free up more of my time to spend on the people who pay me. So what else do I need to do to better leverage what I already have?"

"Ah, patience, my boy. We're not quite done with the segmentation phase yet."

"You're kidding, right? What else could we possibly segment?"

"The next step is to take the 'know your book' concept to an entirely new level by completing a demographic segmentation of your book."

"I've never heard of that. What do you mean?"

"In this next step, you'll explore the demographics of your book. You're going to look for common denominators and anomalies among your clients. Uncovering these will help you spot trends, niches, and methods of conducting business that are natural to you. The demographics of your book will also give you tremendous insight into exactly what components will likely be the most profitable *to* leverage."

"I'm still not sure I follow you," I said.

"All right, tell me, who is your ideal client?"

I grinned. "That's easy. Someone with over $1 million in investable assets who takes my advice and is in a fee-based platform."

I could see the humor in his eyes as though he'd anticipated my response. "Yes, but who is that person really? How old are they? Where do they live? What are their interests? How did you get them as a client? Using the demographics hidden in your book, you can clarify exactly who your ideal client is and how to reach them."

I realized I didn't really know who my ideal client was at all. Sure, I could say they were between 50 and 65 years old, but that's about all I knew for sure. "Okay, I can see the value in that. So what do I do?"

"Begin the demographic process with an age segmentation of the book. Birds of a feather flock together! This is especially true of age segments. This will become increasingly important as we begin leveraging the book for referrals."

"I'm sure you have an age-tier breakdown in mind. Am I right?"

He smiled. "My suggestion would be
- Over 80
- 66–79
- 50–65
- 40–49
- Under 40

"For joint accounts, use the age of the primary decision maker, and for custodial accounts, naturally you'd use the age of the custodian. I'm sure your firm has a filtering mechanism that would allow you to streamline the process?"

"Yes, they do." I'd used it a lot in the past for birthday and Medicare lists.

"Good. For each age tier, keep track of assets, revenue, and the number in each client tier (A, B+, B, C, D). Once you've completed that process, calculate each age tier's ROA. Although advisors usually have some general idea of the age of their book, they're not always accurate in their assumptions. However, when client ages are broken down into age tiers, it becomes much more useful information. And when the ROA is done by age tier, a clearer vision of your ideal client begins to emerge."

"I've never even thought about slicing and dicing the book this much before," I admitted.

Victor continued, "You should also look for anomalies. For example, you may discover that you have more assets in the 66–79 and over 80 age tiers, but your ROA and revenue are higher in the 50–65 age tier. As you look closer, you may find that your older tiers tend to be buy-and-hold clients, whereas your 50–65 age tier tends to generate more fee-based business. This becomes valuable information when you're deciding how to allocate your time, energy, *and* marketing money."

"I'll take more of that 50–65 age tier!" I declared enthusiastically.

"Let's take it a step further. What if you find that your assets, revenue, and ROA are all highest in your 66–79 age tier but when you examine this more closely, you realize you have little or no relationship with the next generation? You may determine that the 66–79 age tier is not only a demographic 'sweet spot' for future marketing efforts but that you also need to develop a plan to capture the next generation."

"This all makes so much sense," I marveled. "I can see how the age segmentation and ROA analysis could help me see trends in my book I didn't even know existed!"

"Right you are, my boy! However, age isn't the only demographic to consider," said Victor with a twinkle in his eye.

"I had a feeling you were going to say that."

"The purpose of the demographic segmentation is actually twofold. Additional demographic components will help you continue to build an ideal client profile. They can also help you uncover natural niches that may exist in your book."

"You mean like a retiree niche," I asked.

"That's a start, but you'll need to be more specific than that to be effective. Niches can be rather large in scope, so when you spot a potential niche, narrow it down to be as specific as possible. The more specific a niche, the more effective it tends to be. There is much more camaraderie and a greater sense of community among smaller, more specific niches. That can make it easier to leverage your niche for referrals later."

"What if there are no niches in my book, or what if there are several," I asked.

"Even if you don't discover any specific niches in your book, which is rather unlikely, the age and book segmentation alone will help clarify your ideal client. And if you uncover several niches, develop a mini-campaign targeting each one. Invariably, one or two will emerge as clearly having more potential. Then you can concentrate your efforts on those."

I had to admire Victor. He was so methodical in his approach to everything—even something as unexciting as book segmentation. "Okay, so now I'm curious. What other demographic components should I look at?"

"Hobbies are one of the most important demographics to consider," he revealed. "Let's say you discover that most of your A and B+ clients are retired. We've already established that retirees as a niche is too broad. Retired golfers or retirees who enjoy fine wine would both be much more powerful niches for you to work."

"Hmm, that makes sense. People are usually pretty passionate about their hobbies."

"Exactly, and they tend to spend quite a bit of money on them as well. Whether the interest is golf, fishing, sailing, or even fine dining, hobbies can break down barriers quickly. They have a way of creating instant rapport. Most advisors have a concentration of some sort of hobby or pastime in their book. Work through your segmentation spreadsheet and note what your best clients' interests are."

As I sat there, I took a mental inventory of my clients. "I know I have a lot of golfers in my book, and I think I have several clients who like fine wine. Do I work all the different hobby niches in my book?"

"Choose the ones you're personally interested in. This can make leveraging your book for new clients more enjoyable. And anything you enjoy doing, you'll do it better *and* more of it," said Victor.

"I think I'd enjoy that wine niche!"

He laughed. "Be creative in your marketing. Hosting events with a hobby focus can be as effective as they are enjoyable. "

"So we have age, ROA, retired or working, hobbies, and probably where they work would be a good one too. Any other demographics I should look for in my book?"

"Neighborhoods are always helpful," he offered. "As you work through your segmentation spreadsheet, look for clients who live in the same neighborhood, subdivision, or retirement community. Even two clients who reside in the same neighborhood could be the beginning of a natural niche for you. Remember, birds of a feather…!"

That would be easy enough to figure out, I thought. I already knew two of my top 10 clients lived in the same subdivision.

And the biggest producer in the office marketed almost exclusively to one of the high-end retiree neighborhoods in the city. I knew it worked.

"Luke, are you still with me?"

"Oh yes, sir, I'm sorry. I was just thinking about the whole neighborhood thing. Wondering why I hadn't done anything like this before now."

"Sometimes a little prodding is all one needs."

"I guess," I sighed.

"The final factor you'll want to analyze as part of your segmentation is the method by which you acquired the clients you wish to replicate. This may help you identify natural ways of doing business."

"What exactly do you mean by natural ways of doing business?"

"Well, let's say you discover that most of your good clients come from referrals, as is usually the case. Then you know that what you need is a systematic approach to generating referral business."

"And I suppose you have a system for that too, right?"

"Absolutely," declared Victor. "In fact, that's one of the most important systems we'll discuss. Plan to spend quite a bit of time on that one."

"I've never done anything proactive when it comes to referrals," I confessed. "I just take what comes."

"Hardly a system, my boy, but don't feel bad. That *is* the approach of most advisors. Allow me to use another example. If you find that a lot of your good clients come from the golf course, then you know that's where you need to focus your marketing efforts. Gathering this type of information is just part of the puzzle. Do you understand now how to use it?"

"Yes, sir, I do. Wow. You weren't kidding when you said a comprehensive book segmentation. These are all things I never sat down and analyzed in my book *ever*, but I can see how all this could give me a much more targeted approach to everything."

"Exactly. Take the information you discover and develop a plan for building your business in a way that is natural for you. Utilize the methodology that's been most successful for you in the past. Develop a profile of your ideal client based on the demographics in your book. Once you've completed that, the foundation for leveraging your book is in place."

"Got it," I said as I finished scribbling some final thoughts in my notebook. At this rate, I might have to splurge on a second "Victor" pen.

Victor stood, and I realized we were done for the day. I glanced at my watch and was shocked to see I'd been there for over three hours.

"Thank you, sir," I said as I threw the notebook and pen into my briefcase. "And thank you for getting to the uh… 'right' person for Cindy."

"As I said, the privilege was mine, Luke."

I hadn't even noticed Henry in the room. He moved toward me with a large yellow envelope in his hand.

"For you, sir," he said, as he presented me with what I assumed was my packet.

Suddenly, without warning, the whole room was consumed with what sounded like a massive lawn mower overhead threatening to mow us all down. The windows rattled, and I whipped around just in time to see a large black helicopter whir past the window toward the back of the house. It passed in an instant, the sound dwindling to steady hum.

"Whoa, what was that?" I blurted.

Victor chuckled. "That, my boy…is my ride."

CHAPTER TO-DO LIST

1. Segment book by tier.

    *   Begin with quantitative analysis using assets and revenue, and assign points accordingly.

    *   Change the breakpoints as necessary based on the nature of your book but maintain the same number of breakpoints and the same number of points per breakpoint.

    *   Assign points based on intangibles.

    *   Total points and assign tiers.

    *   Segment using A, B+, B, C, and D tiers.

2. Segment book by age.

    *   Over 80

    *   66–79

    *   50–65

    *   40–49

    *   Under 40

3. Segment book demographically.

    *   Look for common denominators and anomalies.

    *   Identify niches within the book.

> ➢ Hobbies

> ➢ Neighborhoods

For Additional Resources, go to:

**www.executivetransformations.com/
plateau2pinnacle-additionalresources**

4. THE ART OF LEVERAGE

"The secret of getting ahead is getting started."
— Mark Twain

I'd been practicing my success ritual faithfully for two weeks, and I had to admit, I was starting to notice a dramatic difference in how I felt—in my whole life really. I hadn't missed breakfast with Aimee and the kids once, and I no longer rushed out of the house frazzled, with a "bagel in my mouth," as Victor had so eloquently put it.

I was getting to the office early, and it was a good thing too. Victor's book segmentation had taken some time, but more than that, it had taken a lot of thought. I had to admit, though, that by the time I finished, I really *did* know my book. I was proud of myself for getting it all done. I don't know if it was the success ritual, my visits with Victor, or getting the book segmentation behind me, but I felt in control for the first time in a long time.

My tires screeched as I almost missed the turn by the peeling mailbox—again. The road to Victor's house was full of twists and turns. I really had to learn to slow down.

My mind drifted back to last week's meeting. Joe was

right. Victor was a business genius, and in my mind, he might just have been the "most interesting man in the world," even though he drank Trappist beer. I'd Googled Trappist beer after my limo ride and turns out it's made by Trappist monks in monasteries, primarily in Belgium. They use profits from the beer to support the monastery and give the rest to charity.

"That, my boy…is my ride." I chuckled as I parked my Infiniti in my usual spot. It wasn't a helicopter, but it was my baby, and I loved it just the same.

I couldn't wait to see what Victor had planned for today. I flew up the stairs and rang the doorbell. Henry answered, promptly as usual.

"Good afternoon, sir." Henry was always gracious. Formal, but gracious.

"Hi, Henry. I'm ready to learn something new today," I declared with a grin.

"Well, you've come to the right place, sir. Right this way. Mr. Guise is waiting for you."

I glanced at my watch. "I'm not late, am I?" I asked. The last thing I wanted was to be late for Victor.

"Oh no, sir. You're right on time," he said as he opened the door to the den.

"Mr. Somers, sir," Henry announced.

Victor was sitting in front of the tall windows, absorbed in whatever he was studying on his laptop. He closed it quickly and turned. "Luke, my boy. How are you?"

"I'm great," I answered enthusiastically.

He motioned for me to take a seat in my favorite chair. "Come, sit down and tell me all about it."

"Well, for starters I got the complete segmentation done—including intangibles and demographics," I declared proudly. "And you were right. Seeing the ROA on those C and D accounts was definitely a catalyst for giving a lot of them away."

"And were there any surprises?"

"As a matter of fact, there were a couple in the B tier,

and both were because of the intangibles. One client maxed out on all of the intangibles especially in the future revenue potential category, so I moved him up to B+ status. The other client was my biggest 'aha' moment. We've always had a good relationship, and she's been a solid B client for years. But I never considered how powerful her sphere of influence was. She's a top divorce attorney in town, president of the Downtown Professional Women's Association, and a major fund-raiser for the Grant-a-Wish Foundation. Any one of those areas would be a great niche to tap into."

"I agree! And what did you discover in your demographic segmentation?"

"I have to admit the whole process was a pretty eye-opening experience for me. First of all, I always thought my book was pretty old — you know, mostly retirees. But when I did the age segmentation, I realized that I actually have more clients in the 50–65 age tier than any other group. And thanks to Joe, I have the start of a longshoremen niche in the book too. That's one I think I could really capitalize on!"

"Excellent job!" Victor seemed genuinely pleased with my report.

"I guess I really didn't know my book as well as I thought I did."

"Ah, but you do now, and today we're going to discuss precisely how to leverage that newfound knowledge. It actually is quite simple. The ability to leverage your existing book for additional assets, revenue, and referrals begins and ends with a structured client service model for each tier of client. Do you have one?"

"Uh, not really," I answered sheepishly. "I know I should, but I'm pretty good about keeping in touch with my clients."

"Then you must have some sort of system to keep track of who you've contacted and when you're due to contact them again?"

"Well, kind of. I have a printout of all my clients and look through it every month to figure out who needs a call."

"I see," said Victor. "So do you believe your clients receive a level of service that sets you apart from the masses?"

"Probably not," I mumbled, as I studied the bamboo floor rather than meet his piercing stare.

"Then begin by becoming a student of your own behavior."

"What the heck does that mean?"

Victor smiled. "If you lack a structured system, begin by observing your current behavior patterns. Evaluate how often you presently contact each tier of client and by what methods. Determine what areas you'd care to expand upon, as well as efforts you may deem no longer necessary for each tier. At that point, you can begin to develop your own client contact schedule."

"That sounds easy enough." I shrugged.

"Always remember, a client contact schedule should accomplish two primary objectives. It should raise the level of service to your existing clients, and it must be sustainable regardless of circumstances."

"So in other words, it has to be something I'll actually do, no matter what."

"Exactly," said Victor.

"I do a good job with my best clients. In fact, I usually talk to them every week. It's the rest of them that's the problem. You have some kind of guidelines for those?"

"Of course," he smirked. "Would you for a moment think otherwise?

"I know. What was I thinking?"

"Your client contact schedule should be personalized to fit you and your clients," he explained. "But I'd be happy to share some general guidelines. First of all, you must treat your A and B+ clients the same. Whatever you choose to do for As, you do for B+s as well. That's important if you want B+s to move up the food chain, so to speak."

He opened a file drawer and pulled out a laminated sheet of paper and handed it to me. I studied the breakdown.

Annual Client Contact Schedule

A and B+ Clients
- Phone calls: 10
  - ➢ 4 check-in calls — assistant if applicable
  - ➢ 3 business-related calls — advisor
  - ➢ 3 non-business-related calls — advisor
- Lunch, dinner, event, or outing: 2
- Plan/Investment/Market review: 2 — advisor
- Extras: 3

B Clients
- Phone calls: 5
  - ➢ 2 check-in calls — assistant if applicable
  - ➢ 2 business-related calls — advisor
  - ➢ 1 non-business-related call — advisor
- Lunch, dinner, event, or outing: 1
- Plan/Investment/Market review: 2 — advisor
- Extras: 2

C Clients
- Phone calls: 1 — assistant if applicable
- Market review: 1 — advisor
  - ➢ Alternative Option: Use a conference-call format open to all C clients; if they have questions concerning their individual holdings, they can call you or your assistant.

D Clients
- Market review: 1 — advisor
  - ➢ Alternative Option: Use a conference-call format open to all D clients; if they have questions concerning their individual holdings, they can call your assistant.

"Wow! This is exactly what I need! I like the idea of doing a market review for C clients using a conference call. I have a question though. What are the check-in calls by the assistant if applicable?"

"Ah," said Victor, "if you have a capable assistant, and unfortunately not every advisor does, the assistant can make the calls as outlined. They're actually quite simple. In the call, the assistant merely asks if the client needs anything at that time. Another possibility is a call to update an item in their client record, such as an e-mail address."

"My assistant works for two other guys besides me. Fortunately, one is semi-retired and doesn't give her a whole lot to do. But the other guy dumps a lot of stuff on her sometimes. So she might not be able to make all the calls, but I know she can at least make some."

"Whatever she can do, delegate it to her," he instructed. "It's important to leverage not only your book but your time as well. Do you understand?"

"Yes, sir," I replied. "Ashley is good with people, and the clients love her, so it makes sense to get her involved."

"Sounds like she's up to the task."

I glanced back at the laminated sheet in front of me. "So what's an extra?"

"Excellent question, my boy! It's been my experience that it's the little things that make a huge difference to people. Therefore, I include them in the client service model. Extras are non-business-related items that you periodically send to a client."

"You mean like a gift?" I asked.

"It can be a small gift," he explained. "But it doesn't have to be. Say for instance, you have a client who loves Labrador retrievers, and who doesn't, by the way?"

"You're right about that," I chimed in. "I have a big white one at home. He's like one of the kids, only better behaved a lot of the time!"

Victor laughed. "Fine dogs, they are. I've had the privilege of owning several over the course of my life."

Funny, I didn't picture him as a Labrador man. He seemed more like a Doberman guy to me. Labs can be so goofy until they grow up a little. I wondered if he was a hunter. Now that I could picture — Victor strolling through a misty field at dawn, rifle in hand, one of those well-trained dogs with total focus by his side.

"So are you a hunter?" I asked.

"Oh no," he answered. "I could never kill an animal."

He smiled and then seemed to drift away to some distant place. He didn't say anything for a long while. I wondered what memory our discussion had triggered. When he spoke, his tone was different, softer.

"My wife was very fond of the breed…preferred the English line," he murmured. "Our dogs were always pets, in the truest sense."

I studied his expression. Its unmistakable sadness told me his wife was gone. There was no way to know if that was due to death or divorce, and I wasn't about to ask. I left him to his memories and waited patiently.

After what seemed like almost a minute, he glanced at me and snapped back to the business at hand.

"So…extras," he resumed. "As I was saying, they can be a small gift but also can be as simple as a newspaper or magazine article. We've established that you have client with an affinity for Labrador Retrievers. So let's say you happen to read an article about a Labrador that heroically saved a drowning child. Make a copy and send it to your client with a personal note that says something along the lines of 'I immediately thought of you when I saw this.'"

"Oh, I get it. Just a little something that shows you were thinking about them."

"Exactly. Those kinds of touches are priceless and bond you to the client on a much deeper level!"

"I can see that, but," I hesitated. "What if I don't know enough about the client's interests to send an extra?

"Ah, 'know your client,' my boy," he mocked. "That's where the Soft Touch Questionnaire can be of assistance."

"What's that?"

"I'm glad you asked," he said, smiling as he pulled out another laminated sheet of paper. "This is not something you send to the client or even review with them over the phone. This is something from which you pull one or two questions to work into your conversation. If you do this each time you speak to them, you'll find that you have all you need to send the extras."

I scanned the sheet and immediately understood what he meant. "Everything You Always Wanted to Know about Clients" was emblazoned across the top of the page, and what followed was a list of questions that would certainly give you lots of ideas for extras.

Everything You Always Wanted to Know about Clients

Children/Grandchildren

Names/Ages/Interests (sports, music, in college, out of college, etc.)

What kinds of things do they like to do with their children or grandchildren?

Pets

Do they like animals?

Any pets?

Pet names?

Do they belong to any clubs or groups focused on their pets?

Do they "show" their pets in any events or competitions?

Reading

What do they like to read? (Fiction, nonfiction, historical novels, travel books, business books, etc.)

What's their favorite bookstore?

Who's their favorite author?

Movies

Do they like movies?

Do they like to go to the theater or rent at home?

What genre of movies do they like?

Who are their favorite actors or actresses?

Music

What kind of music do they like?

Do they listen to music on their phone or iPod?

Do they like live music?

Who is their favorite group or musician?

Foods/Drinks

Favorite foods?

Favorite restaurants?

What foods don't they like?

Do they have any food allergies?

What are their favorite nonalcoholic drinks? (Coffee, tea, Coke, Pepsi, diet or regular)

What's their favorite alcoholic drink?

Favorite sweet or snack they don't allow themselves very often? (Make a point to have it on hand for meetings/appointments)

Sports

Do they participate in sports? Which sport?

Are they a member of any clubs? (Tennis, country club, health club)

Do they like football, baseball, basketball, hockey?

Do they follow pro teams or college teams?

What teams are their favorites?

Travel

Do they like to travel?

Is there anywhere they have not been that they would like to go?

Do they have a vacation home?

What's their favorite destination?

Charity

Do they have a favorite charity?

Do they have a cause that they believe in or support?

Do they intend to gift or leave any money to a charity?

Has that been outlined in a will or trust?

Community

Are they on any specific community boards or groups?

Do they support any local groups? (Theater, symphony, opera)

Are they involved in any church groups?

Technology

Have they embraced technology?

E-mail?

iPad?

Smartphone?

Do they text?

Do they play any computer games?

Are they on social media? What's their favorite network?

"Wow! This really is everything you could ever want to know about clients," I proclaimed. "So what's the easiest way to keep track of all this?"

"That depends entirely on you. If you're the technology sort, you can attach the document to the client file. Then add a reminder so you remember to pull questions when you're speaking with them. I've also known advisors to copy a number of these sheets and place them in a binder. When a client calls, they simply pull one and begin a sheet on that client. They then file the sheets in the binder alphabetically. The binder is on their desk at all times, so they remember to pull the client's sheet when they're speaking to them."

"That works, but I have a question for you."

"Fire away, my boy."

"What about birthdays and holidays? In the past I sent birthday cards when I remembered, but I didn't exactly remember all the time. I am pretty good about getting holiday cards out in December. What do you think about cards, and do they count as touches?"

"I think holiday cards are fine," he answered. "And in fact, if you've sent them in the past, clients almost expect to receive them. Basically, you have two choices with holiday cards. You can send out Thanksgiving cards. This distinguishes you from many advisors, although this *is* becoming a more popular option of late.

"If you choose to send a Happy Holidays card of some sort, I would suggest you time it so it's quite possibly their first card of the season and arrives immediately after Thanksgiving. And by the way, I would not count it as a touch. They still require a call. You're almost like family when you call around the holidays."

"Okay. But what about birthdays?"

"Now birthdays are another subject entirely. I personally am not a real proponent of birthday cards. I think a phone call is far more personal and does count as a touch."

"Why don't you like birthday cards?"

"It's not that I dislike them. But think about the birthday cards you receive from your real estate agent or your automobile salesman. Where do they go? I know mine go immediately in the trash. However, when someone takes the time to call me on my birthday, I notice."

"I guess that's true when you think about it. So when is your birthday?" I asked mischievously.

"Ah, my boy. Not much gets past you, does it?" He smiled but didn't answer.

When it was obvious he wasn't going to, I decided to move on. "What are your thoughts on events? We haven't talked about those."

"Although events do have a place in a client service discussion, I tend to think of them more as campaigns or as an added value you offer to clients. You may choose to handle the touches surrounding an event somewhat differently. This is simply my opinion.

"If you're calling to invite a client to an event or inform them of an upcoming event, that contact is most definitely counted as a touch because it's proactive on your part. However, if they show up to the event, it is not counted as a touch because it's not something you have control over. Follow-up calls after the event are critical to its success and proactive in nature. Therefore, they would count as a client service touch."

"So what you're saying is anything that's proactive counts as a touch. Anything that I don't have control over doesn't. Right?"

"Correct, but ultimately, your client service model is a reflection of you, not me, so *you* decide what's counted as a touch and what's not. What I've given you today are guidelines to take and make your own. Tailor them to you and your style so you'll actually use them. Develop habits that are sustainable. The greatest service model in the world is of no value if you won't or can't implement it. Do you understand?"

I nodded. "Yes, sir."

"Good." He shifted in his chair. "This brings us to the final two pieces of the leverage puzzle, and they are critical to your success. They are automation and implementation."

"You've given me some fantastic information today, but to be honest, I'm not sure where to even start when it comes to implementation," I admitted. "I don't want this to be another great idea that I don't implement, so I'm all ears."

"The first thing to do is develop your client contact template for each tier of client. This can be in spreadsheet form or in a word document. Put it on a single sheet of paper so you can laminate it and keep it handy. Both you and your assistant will refer to it often so make sure she has a copy as well. It might look something like this."

He pulled out a laminated sheet of paper and handed it to me. Each tier of client had its own section, and all of the contacts were laid out very specifically.

Sample Monthly Client Contact Schedule

A/B+ Clients

Jan: Sales asst. calls to set up review; advisor completes review

Feb: Advisor call

Mar: Advisor call; extra sent

Apr: Sales asst. call

May: Dinner, lunch, or outing; advisor sets up and completes

Jun: Advisor call; extra sent

Jul: Sales asst. calls to set up review; advisor completes review

Aug: Advisor call

Sep: Advisor call; extra sent

Oct: Sales asst. call

Nov: Dinner, lunch, or outing; advisor sets up and completes

Dec: Advisor call

B Clients

Feb: Dinner, lunch, or outing; advisor sets up and completes

Mar: Sales asst. calls to set up review; advisor completes review

Apr: Advisor call

May: Extra sent

Jun: Advisor call

Sep: Sales asst. calls to set up review; advisor completes review

Oct: Extra sent

Dec: Advisor call

C and D Clients

Feb: Advisor sends e-mail blast inviting all Cs and Ds to a Market Review and Update conference call

Aug: Sales asst. calls (if applicable) C clients only

He paused to give me time to review the sheet, and then he continued, "A few things to remember as you're setting up your template. Remember, you always want to treat A and B+ clients the same in hopes of moving B+ clients to A status."

"So I'd probably want to set up the A/B+ template first and work the B, C, and D contacts in around that, right?"

"Excellent thinking, my boy," he beamed. "It's also of utmost importance that your calls and touches are staggered based on your client contact schedule and the number of clients you have in each tier. The last thing you want is for your client contact schedule to be unachievable because you've scheduled 75 calls for one day!"

"No, that definitely would not work."

"However, with that said, I would plan on having each tier of client on the same contact schedules in the same months as I've laid out here. This allows you to get in that tier's 'zone,' so to speak. You'll find each tier will tend to have similar issues, plans, and investments, and it will be easier if you are accomplishing similar things for a similar group in the same month. Do you understand?"

"Absolutely. That's a really good idea."

"Now notice," he continued. "One of your A/B+ dinner, lunch, or outing touches is in November. Personally, I think it's nice to have one of these touches for your A/B+ clients before Thanksgiving as a sort of thank-you outing. The other one is just spaced six months from that month."

"I like that idea. It really is kind of an appreciation outing when you do it in November like that. And that's exactly what I want my A and B+ clients to feel—appreciated!"

"That," he emphasized, "is what you're trying to

achieve in your client service model. You're trying to build an experience for your clients that they will appreciate and remember. As I said in the beginning, your ability to leverage your book for additional assets, referrals, and revenue begins and ends with the quality and consistency of your service model. It's also your golden opportunity to distinguish yourself from the masses, transform clients into advocates, and increase the quantity and quality of referrals."

"I'm really anxious to get started on this client service model stuff. It's something I've done loosely on and off for years, but I can see now, it's time I made it formal and a habit."

"That's why the automation step is such a critical one. Segmenting your book and establishing your tiered client service model are great first steps, but unless you have the process automated, chances are it'll be one that falls by the wayside after just a couple of weeks. Automation helps you develop a pattern of consistency, which is the foundation of superior client service."

"I agree with that, but how do I take *all* you've given me today and automate it into my contact management system?"

"All right, listen carefully."

"Please tell me this will be in my packet today."

"Indeed it will. You don't think I'd leave something as important as your client service model to chance or memory, do you?"

"Whew. Glad to hear that."

He continued, "So you have your laminated client contact template. Next, based on the client contact template you've developed, figure out how many calls you need to make each day in order to get all your contacts in. Once you come up with that number, make it a point to work through your A/B+ and B clients with a phone call in their designated months. Then either you or your assistant set the recurring calls and tasks from the date of that initial phone call. By setting a client's recurring activities as you speak to them, client contacts are staggered and, therefore, manageable."

"So let me make sure I've got this. Say I have 20 A/B+ clients and 40 B clients and I'm starting the client service model in September. That means I need to make 20 A/B+ calls and send out 20 extras that month. So I can make one call a day, and if I want to send all my extras out on Fridays, I'll need to send out five extras per Friday in September, right?"

"Correct," he confirmed.

"And say I call George Smith on September 7. I give my assistant his name and tell her he's an A. She looks at the client contact template and sets all recurring tasks and calls from that September 7 date, right?"

"That's it!"

"Okay, so now October rolls around, and I have to send out extras to B clients. I have 40 B clients, and I'm only sending out extras on Fridays," I said slowly. "Ten extras sound like a lot to get out every Friday." Looking down at the laminated template he'd given me, a lightbulb suddenly went off. "I could send out five per Friday for two months because I don't have any to get out the following month in November!"

"Now you're thinking!"

"Then I just give the list of five Bs each Friday to my assistant to enter the recurring tasks and calls, and she can set one call for each day. Even though it'll take me two months to get through all 40 Bs, that's still not too many calls to make even if I overlap an A/B+ month like December. This is really cool!"

"And you'll find when you're proactively making the calls to clients on a consistent basis, you'll have far fewer incoming calls to bog you down," he added.

"This makes more sense than anything I've ever tried before. I can't thank you enough. You broke it all down into a process that's not overwhelming. I think I could actually do this!"

"You're welcome, my boy. I believe you're on your way to leveraging that book of yours far more effectively. However, there's one last thing, and it's very important."

"What's that?"

His expression suddenly changed again, and he got very serious. "Once your client contact schedule is automated, you must be diligent in keeping up with your task list each day," he said sternly. "I recommend that you also establish a cleanup block on either Thursday or Friday to handle all the tasks for the week that you were unable to handle previously for whatever reason. Ideally, you want to begin each week with a clear calendar and little or no carryover from the previous week.

"Also, this is all about you being proactive. If you call a client and you're unable to get in touch with them, leave a message. Regardless of whether or not they return the call, it counts as your touch. You proactively reached out to them. It's their choice whether to call you back or not."

"Okay. I'm ready to get this thing started!"

"Remember, Luke, markets may be out of your control, but client service is not. It's important in this business to focus on what you can control. Just establishing the system and beginning to implement it is going to make you feel more proactive, more in control. This is something you need to do for your clients and for yourself."

"Well, I have my work cut out for me," I said. "So next week?"

"Next week it is. Same day and time. I'll look forward to hearing all about your progress."

When I turned to leave, Henry was waiting patiently at the door, packet in hand. *How does he do that?* I wondered. *How does he know the precise moment we're done every week? Another of Victor's mysteries I guess.*

"No helicopter today?" I asked Victor as I was leaving.

He smiled. "Not today, my boy. I thought I'd just order a pizza tonight."

CHAPTER TO-DO LIST

1. Create your own client contact schedule by tier and laminate.

    - Start by being a student of your own behavior and what you're currently doing in the way of client service.

        ➢ What do you want to do more of and less of in the way of client service?

    - Develop a client service model that raises your current level of service and is sustainable.

    - It should be personalized to fit you and your book.

    - If you have a capable assistant, include him or her in some simple client service touches.

    - Delegate whenever possible to leverage your time as well as your book.

    - Include extras—the little things that make a big difference to clients.

    - Always treat A and B+ clients the same in terms of client service.

    - Both you and your assistant should have a laminated copy on your desk and refer to it often.

    - In order for touches to clients to count, they must be proactive and in your control.

2. Develop a Soft Touch Questionnaire (STQ).

- Plan on pulling one or two questions to work into conversations with clients.

  ➤ This allows you to increase your level of service by knowing your client better.

  ➤ This allows you to be in a better position to send extras to clients regularly

- Keep your STQ handy at all times so you remember to use it.

  ➤ Attach it to the client file in your contact management system with some sort of reminder to pull it up when talking to clients.

  ➤ If you prefer hard copies, use a binder set up alphabetically with an STQ sheet for each client. Keep on your desk at all times with some sort of reminder to use.

3. Automate your client contact schedule.

- Start with your A and B+ clients and make your initial phone call.

  ➤ Voice mails count because they are proactive on your part regardless of whether you receive a callback from the client.

  ➤ Have your assistant set all recurring activities from that initial contact so your contacts are staggered.

4. Implement flawlessly.

- Establish a cleanup block on Thursday or Friday for all the contacts and touches that were not made during the week for whatever reason.

- Make it your goal to begin each week with little or no pending contacts or touches from the previous week.

For Additional Resources, go to:

**www.executivetransformations.com/
plateau2pinnacle-additionalresources**

5. REFERRALS

"When it is obvious that the goals cannot be reached, don't adjust the goals, adjust the action steps."

— Confucius

It was hard to believe another week had gone by already. I pulled into Victor's driveway feeling exhausted and exhilarated. I couldn't remember the last time I'd worked as hard as I had this week. As usual, Victor was right. Just putting together the system and starting to implement it *had* made me feel more in control, and I did get a lot more done. I felt empowered! It was great to be making outgoing calls again and not just reacting.

I drifted back to when I used to dream of being a million-dollar producer. When we first got in the business, Ben and I just always assumed we'd get there, but it had been a long time since I'd had those thoughts and actually believed them. It felt like a lifetime ago — before 2008 and well before I hit my perennial plateau. When Ben died, I thought they were gone for good, but my meetings with Victor had brought them back to life. I knew we were building the foundation I needed to get there.

Halfway up the stairs, I stopped and turned around. I inhaled deeply and took in the magnificence of the Madison estate. Even my Infiniti looked ridiculously out of place in front of Victor's sprawling home. I knocked on the door enthusiastically and felt that same rush of excitement I did every Thursday as I waited for Henry's formal but warm greeting.

He answered with his usual promptness and led me back to what had become my favorite classroom ever. Victor was busy scribbling something on a tattered yellow pad.

"So how's my favorite student today?" he asked, as he finished off some final scribbles. I wondered what he had in store for me today.

"I'm fantastic and feeling much more in control than I did last week!"

"Ah, then you must have followed my suggestions."

"I did, and I now officially have a client contact system."

"Good for you, my boy. Now comes the hard part." His tone changed to serious in a flash. "You must implement it flawlessly from this moment forward. Therein lies your biggest challenge *and* your greatest reward."

I nodded and found myself hanging on his every word.

"There will be days when implementation will be tough whether for market reasons or personal ones—it doesn't matter. You must *always* do it anyway. You must be willing to do what others don't to gain what others won't. That, my boy, is what separates the great from the mediocre. Do you understand?"

"Yes, sir, I do."

And I did understand. I knew exactly what had kept me from reaching my potential in the past. I'd get all excited about something and would implement it for a couple of weeks or so, but then the excitement wore off, and I'd go back to my old habits.

I was a master avoider, and I'd shift into avoidance mode until the next great thing came along. That was my pattern and had been, for most of my career. I'd grown comfortable and complacent, and I knew it.

As if reading my mind, Victor looked me straight in the eye and asked, "So what is your plan for overcoming your inevitable avoidance when it arises?"

I knew he probably didn't expect me to have much of an answer. But I'd actually thought about that very question all week, almost anticipating it.

"Well, it's going to take active mind control on my part. I know that much. Unfortunately, avoidance has become a bad habit of mine and one I'm very good at. So when I feel like procrastinating or blowing it off, first I'm going to notice and become aware of what I'm doing — or not doing. Then I'm going to look at my goals for the day and tell myself that I just have to call for 12 minutes. That's all. I can do anything for 12 minutes. I think once I start I'll be okay and probably end up making calls for more than 12 minutes."

There was a long silence until finally he said, "Mmm, 12 minutes. Interesting. If you don't mind me asking, how did you arrive at 12 minutes?"

Ha! I thought. I'd surprised him with that one. I could barely hide the satisfaction in my voice as I told him the story.

"A couple of years ago my wife wanted me to go to yoga with her. Let's just say I wasn't overly excited about the idea. She gave me this yoga video to start with, and it was 12 minutes long. She let me know in no uncertain terms that I could do anything for 12 minutes. I guess she was right because I'm still at it two years later, only I do it for longer than 12 minutes now. I figured if it worked with yoga, it could work in my business too!"

He cocked his head to one side like he had a way of doing when he was concentrating on something. He seemed to be pondering my answer.

"Your wife sounds like a very wise woman. Wise for pushing you to begin yoga and wiser still for her 12-minute rule. I like that very much. If you don't object, I may have occasion to use it myself sometime." He smiled.

"I'd be flattered, sir. But I have to say, I can't imagine you avoiding anything."

Victor chuckled. "Ah, my boy, don't kid yourself. I *am* human after all. And avoidance, I'm afraid, is part of human nature."

"I guess that's true." I shrugged.

"Now, what do you think is at the root of your avoidance? Why do you do it?"

I stared out the window at nothing in particular as I carefully considered his question. Finally I realized I didn't have an answer. I'd thought about why in the past but always seemed to find a convenient distraction to avoid digging deeper and discovering the real why.

"I guess I don't know," I answered.

Victor nodded. "There are a multitude of reasons advisors avoid making calls to clients and prospects. Some do it because they feel they shouldn't have to make the calls. Some because they're embarrassed to make the calls. Some because they don't want to be disappointed when they get the inevitable rejection. And some because they feel as though they're bothering or interrupting the person when they call. So what's *your* poison?"

"I guess a combination of the last two—I don't want to be disappointed, and I don't like bothering people," I mumbled.

"We're talking about this now because you're in a contact sport, and your ability to consistently implement contact, whether it's with clients or prospects, is of utmost importance. In fact, it's critical to your success. And both of your reasons can be cured by a single antidote."

"What?" I asked hopefully.

"Conviction! Conviction in who you are, what you do for

people, and what you charge to do it. Conviction sells, my boy! And do you know how to build it?"

"Apparently not," I answered.

"You build it by doing exactly what we're doing—systematizing your business. This journey you've chosen to undertake positions you light-years ahead of other advisors in terms of efficiency of operation. Furthermore, each new system we build adds to your professionalism in the eyes of the client, but more importantly, in your eyes."

"That's already started to happen," I observed.

"Your conviction will grow with each new system—if and only if you implement it consistently. As you implement each of these systems, you become more proactive and in control. The more you feel *you're* the one in control, the more professional you feel, and the more conviction you will build. When you have conviction in something, you can't wait to share it with others. Would you agree?"

Victor was right about that. I nodded enthusiastically.

"You no longer feel you're bothering someone, but rather, you feel it's your duty and obligation to share your ideas with them. If someone tells you no, you're not disappointed for yourself, you're disappointed for them! Conviction is an energy, an aura if you will, and it's contagious. If you have it, your clients will have it too. They'll feel the same enthusiasm about what they're doing that you do!"

I so wanted to believe what he was saying was true. Could it really be that simple? Was conviction my missing link all these years? I was mesmerized with his words.

"Have you ever noticed how clients are usually a lot like their advisors? If an advisor is a nice guy, he tends to have nice clients. If the advisor is obnoxious, usually his clients are too. In most cases, your clients' energy will mirror your own. Always remember, my boy, conviction sells! That is your new mantra. Do you understand?"

"Yes, sir!" I could feel my own conviction and enthusiasm building as he spoke. He was right. It was contagious.

"Conviction sells! I like it. It will be my new mantra!" I couldn't wait for whatever was next.

"So what are we going to talk about today?" I asked as I took out my notebook and Victor pen. I prepared what was becoming my Olympic-caliber writing hand for the afternoon marathon by stretching it several times. And then we were off.

"Today is an important day because today we build a complete referral process."

My conviction suddenly faded. I'd never been good at asking for referrals. Sure, they trickled in from time to time, but it definitely was not because I asked.

I felt like I did a pretty good job for my "A" clients and that they'd give me a steady stream of referrals based on that. I always wanted to be one of those guys whose business grew exclusively through referrals, but nothing like that ever happened for me.

Victor interrupted my thoughts with the one question I always dreaded: "So do you ask for referrals?"

I paused, and realizing there was no escape, I reluctantly replied, "No, I don't." My face burned with embarrassment.

"Good!"

"What?" There was no hiding the shock on my face.

"It's good you don't ask for referrals," he said matter-of-factly. "When you ask someone for a referral, it's awkward for you and for them, and you're asking them to do all the work."

"What do you mean?" I asked, still stunned.

"You're asking them to basically think up someone to refer to you with no advance notice or warning and with no idea at all of what you're looking for in a referral. It's rare to get a referral by asking cold like that, and if by chance you happen to get one, it's usually not the kind of person you'd care to have as a client anyway. Am I correct?"

"Well, I suppose that's true, but I never really thought about it like that. I was always too busy beating myself up for never asking."

"Well, you can stop that too, my boy, because you're about to learn the key to having a steady stream of referrals and introductions each month and a whole process built around it."

"I don't mean to sound disrespectful, sir, but I wish I had a dollar for every referral system that promised that. Nothing in the referral department has *ever* worked for me at all, much less produce a steady stream of anything, except disappointment."

Victor smiled. "Do you trust me, Luke?"

"Implicitly, sir."

"Then you need to trust my referral system, do you not?"

I looked at Victor. Here was a man who had helicopters picking him up in the afternoon, for god's sake. And let's not forget how he fixed the problem with Ben's book. What reason could I possibly have for not trusting his referral system?

"Yes, sir, I guess I do."

"Do you know what the secret is to getting that steady stream of referrals and introductions you always wanted?"

"I have absolutely no idea," I said truthfully.

"Referral conditioning," he answered with a twinkle in his eye.

"Okay." I made no effort to hide my skepticism. "What does that mean exactly?"

"It means the average person, unless they've been in sales before, would have to have someone approach them on the street and say, 'I just won the lottery, who's your financial advisor?' for them to even *think* in terms of referrals."

I thought about that for several seconds. "Well, that's certainly true of my clients. I always thought if I did a good job for people, the referrals would come, but that never really happened."

"Do you know why?" He paused briefly and then continued without waiting for a response, "It's because you never conditioned them to think in terms of referrals. *It's all about conditioning!*

"The last thing in the world I want you to do is walk around groveling to anyone who crosses your path, asking them to please pass along your business card should the subject of investments ever arise. You and I both know that doesn't work. My approach, on the other hand, does. It has four components to it, *and* it's far less stressful than asking everyone you know for referrals."

Now he had my attention. "Well, that sounds good to me. I *hate* asking people for referrals!"

"I assumed that—since you don't like to be disappointed or bother people." He laughed. "Three of the four components are simply passive conditioning techniques that require very little effort on your part. The other piece of the puzzle is the proactive piece, and that's what we're going to discuss first."

I had to admit I was curious. What kind of system could Victor have possibly devised that would produce a steady stream of referrals or introductions without having to really ask? It sounded a little too good to be true. But then again, everything he'd shared with me so far had worked just like he said it would. If he really did have a system for referrals that actually worked, how huge would that be for my business!

He stared at me for a moment as if reading my mind. When he continued, he had the tone of a historian. "Financial advisors across the country are now and have always been on a never-ending quest to discover *the* magic bullet, the Holy Grail if you will, for building their book through referrals.

"However, as we've established, the vast majority of advisors never ask for referrals but rather take what comes and practically throw a party if they get one—regardless of quality. In fact, only about 2–3% of financial advisors have *any* kind of systematic approach for generating referral business."

Two to three percent? That couldn't be right. Then I started thinking about my own office of 27 advisors and realized the figure was probably pretty accurate.

Before meeting Victor, that stat would have probably made me feel better — like I was normal, but not anymore. Ever since I met him, my attitude was different. Even Aimee had noticed. She said I seemed more confident, poised, and in control. It wasn't just my business that was changing. I was starting to change — I could feel it.

"So what's the answer? Tell me what works and I'll do it."

I wanted and needed a system for referrals, but it had to be one I'd actually use or it was worthless. I held my breath, hoping and praying Victor's system would somehow work for me.

"The proactive part of that answer is something I like to call my Referral Detective Strategy©," he said, practically glowing with excitement.

"At this point, I'm willing to try anything. How does it work?"

"It's very low tech. In fact, the only purchase necessary is a notebook to your liking. It should have blank pages. Optimally, it should be pocket calendar or checkbook sized so it can fit in your coat pocket or back pocket. And," he said very seriously, "you must carry it with you at all times — even when you're not at work. Do you understand?"

"Yes, sir." I nodded, faking enthusiasm and unsure of where he was going with all of this.

Satisfied, he continued, "Most advisors have radar when someone is mentioned within the context of an investment or business-related conversation. Would you agree?"

I thought about how I typically respond when I'm talking to a client about business and they mention someone in the conversation. "I guess that's true. I usually do ask a couple of questions about the person."

"Then what do you do?"

"Well, usually nothing," I confessed.

"What about when someone is mentioned in a non-business-related conversation?"

"You mean when I'm just talking to somebody about their kids or football or something?"

"Yes. What do you do when people are mentioned in all the casual conversations you have within in the course of a day, a week, or a month?

"I'm not sure I even notice," I answered, wondering what he was after.

"Precisely! I guarantee, there are some real gems in terms of prospects that are mentioned to you within the course of all those plain, run-of-the-mill conversations you have every day. These are *gifts*, my boy, and you're overlooking them. Many have tremendous potential! So we're going to begin by training your ear to hear these and, most importantly, be diligent about recording them in your Referral Detective Notebook."

"So what do I put in the notebook besides their name, and how am I going to start noticing them?"

"Excellent questions! Each entry in the notebook should have the date of the conversation, the source—that's the person you're talking to—and as many notes as you can remember about the person mentioned. You don't even need a proper name. You just need enough in your notes so that when you go back to the source for the introduction, they'll know to whom you are referring."

I must have looked puzzled because he quickly added, "Let me give you an example. Suppose you're talking to your client, Sam Jones, later today, and Mr. Jones tells you he went skiing with his best buddy last weekend and they had a great time. He also tells you that they go every year."

At this point, Victor got excited, almost animated. I listened and watched in disbelief as his level of excitement over referrals, of all things, continued to build.

"In your Referral Detective Notebook," he continued, "you're going to write today's date. The source is Sam Jones, and in this case, he didn't furnish a proper name. So in your notes, you're going to write 'went skiing with best buddy, does it once a year.' Are you with me?"

"I guess so. I have what goes in the entry—date, source, and notes—but how am I ever going to remember to notice when people are mentioned in all the conversations I have in a day?"

Victor glanced at me slyly and began, "That's probably the most difficult part of the entire system, but it just so happens I have a few tricks for you!"

"That doesn't surprise me." I smiled. His enthusiasm was so over the top it was starting to rub off on me.

He continued, "The first thing you need to remember is that a Referral Detective Entry can come from anyone and is not limited to just clients. Entries can come from clients, prospects, business associates, people you do business with personally, friends, or relatives. They can come from anywhere. That's why you need to have your notebook with you at all times."

"Okay, so that's why it's checkbook sized, right?"

"Correct. The second thing to remember is that your Referral Detective Notebook should be sitting on your desk right next to your phone whenever you're in the office. As soon as you hang up the phone after speaking with anyone, use that as your cue to do what I call the 7-Second Scan."

"So what's that?"

"Take seven seconds to scan the conversation and ask yourself if anyone was mentioned. When you're out on appointments, take the book out of your coat pocket and leave it on your car seat so you have to pick it up to get in the car. That's your cue to do the 7-Second Scan. Whenever someone is mentioned, make an entry in your notebook immediately or you will surely forget. Are you still with me?"

"Yes, sir, I'm with you." I grinned. This was something I could actually do. How awesome would it be to have a referral system I actually used! I looked Victor right in the eye and asked, "So what other tricks do you have up your sleeve?"

He must have sensed my level of excitement building because he grinned right back and said, "Bait questions! These are questions that when asked, invariably spark entries. They can be questions as simple as 'What did you guys do last weekend? Do you have any big plans this weekend? Are you going to the game on Sunday?' And there's always a holiday around the corner that you can use to your benefit by asking, 'What are you doing for Thanksgiving? What did you do for the Fourth of July?' These kinds of questions almost always generate an entry, and they establish you as interested and attentive at the same time. If you can become proficient at bait questions, you'll have no trouble getting entries every day."

"So how many entries should I be shooting for in a week?"

"If you can average just two entries a day or 10 a week, you'd have approximately 40 entries a month. Even if 80–90% of them drop out for whatever reason, that still equates to four to eight good, solid introductions per month. Most advisors would be ecstatic to have four to eight introductions a month. Would you agree?"

"I know I would! But what do you mean drop out?"

"I'm glad you asked because that brings me to another important point. The Referral Detective Strategy works because it's based on our favorite premise — the old 'birds of a feather flock together' concept. If you have a million-dollar client, chances are they're associating with others close to their own socioeconomic status.

"However, do *not* get in the habit of making judgment calls while collecting entries. By judgment calls, I mean thinking 'This is a good one, this is a bad one.' I want you to take down any and all entries. The time for judgment calls comes when you put together your Referral Detective Hit List at the end of every month."

"Referral Detective Hit List, huh? Sounds dangerous." I laughed. "So what exactly is that?"

"At the end of each month, review all your entries and choose what you think are your best opportunities. This determination will be based on your notes about the entry and the quality of the source. Remember, birds of a feather flock together. If the source is a high-net-worth client, chances are good that the person they mentioned might also be high net worth. If you know the source doesn't have any money, there's a strong probability that the entry will be marginal at best, and this entry may be dropped. Go through all your entries and make a list of all the ones you think may have potential. Then it's time to determine your next step."

"Which is?"

"The next step depends on the personality of the source and your style as an advisor. Some sources tend to be more social by nature than others, or they have hobbies that lend themselves to social outings like golf or wine tasting. Likewise, some advisors have a very social relationship with their clients. Others do not. They do their job at the office and would prefer to not even run into their clients on the street. How you handle this step is primarily dependent on your style and that of the source."

"That makes sense." Actually everything he was saying made a lot of sense. Four to eight potential introductions every month sounded career changing to me.

There was no stopping him now. "Let's return to your source, Sam Jones," he continued. "Mr. Jones obviously enjoys skiing. If social is your style, you may want to make your next step some sort of outing centered around what you know the source and your potential introduction like to do. In this case, you'd call your source and say something like 'Sam, I know you like to ski. Let's plan a trip up the mountain for a day. You know, you mentioned that buddy of yours you went skiing with last month. Do you think he's someone I should meet? Why don't you see if he wants to join us?'"

He was smooth. I'd give him that. I decided to play the devil's advocate. "So what if he says the guy doesn't have any money or he's a jerk?"

"Regardless of how he answers the question, it allows you to gather more information about the potential introduction. If Mr. Jones's response is positive, then voila! You have yourself an introduction. Should he respond that his friend probably couldn't or wouldn't join you for skiing and you still think he has potential, then put Mr. Jones in an advisory role and ask what he thinks would be the best way to meet his friend. Most people love to give advice and, in many cases, are willing to help.

"Now if Mr. Jones tells you that his skiing buddy is a great friend but would be difficult to work with or doesn't have any money, then you're probably better off just taking Mr. Jones skiing and consider it a goodwill bonding experience with your client. However, if he tells you that his friend already works with someone or if Mr. Jones is vague, then you probably want to go ahead and invite him. After all, if he's working with someone else, that's actually good news because you know he has money. I would treat that as a positive response."

The whole system was beautifully simple. I considered myself a pretty social guy but not all the time and not with everyone I know. So I asked, "What if social isn't your style or is only your style sometimes? How would you handle the same scenario without the ski trip?"

Without missing a beat, Victor responded, "In that case you'd call your source and say something along the lines of 'Hey, Sam, a couple of weeks ago you mentioned that buddy of yours who you go skiing with every year. Do you think he's someone I should meet?'

"Again, you want to listen carefully to his response. If he responds negatively, you probably want to forget the meeting. You can thank him for his honesty but use the opportunity to lightheartedly condition him a little more to think in terms of referrals."

"So how exactly do you do that?"

"You might say something like 'I appreciate your honesty. I wanted to ask you about him because you know how much I enjoy working with you. In fact, I'm always looking for clients just like you. If I could, I'd clone you!'

"Notice how everything I said was casual and light. The more casual and calm you are, the more casual and calm the source will be. I know you've heard the term 'transference,' but do you know what the actual definition of the word is?"

I thought for a moment. "Isn't it where you transfer something like an attitude to somebody else?"

"Pretty close." Victor nodded. "The technical definition is a phenomenon characterized by the unconscious redirection of feelings from one person to another. Usually advisors are so stressed out about asking for referrals, the client senses that energy, and they become stressed as well."

"And that's a big reason they don't get the referral, right?"

"Exactly," said Victor. "The result is usually no referral or a low-quality referral at best. So what is the moral of the story?"

"Hmm. I'd say the more casual and calm you can be during the Hit List stage of the Referral Detective Strategy, the more productive the strategy will be for you."

"Good. Now, let's get back to Sam, shall we?"

"Sure," I replied.

"Suppose he gives you a somewhat positive response to your question about whether you should meet his friend. Or perhaps he tells you that he knows his friend is already working with someone. How will you respond?"

"I guess I would say something like 'It never hurts to

have a second opinion,' and I'd ask Sam to pass along my business card."

I knew my answer was pretty lame as soon as the words left my mouth. Victor immediately validated my feeling with a look of disappointment.

"Oh, my boy," he sighed. "Rather cliché-ish and ineffective, wouldn't you say?"

"I know." I hesitated briefly, now wishing I'd said nothing at all. "So what would you say?"

"Well, first of all, I would never say, 'Please pass along my business card!' It's an absolute waste of breath. The probability of anyone, with the exception of perhaps your mother, passing along your business card is slim. And if by some miracle someone did pass along your business card, the chances of the recipient actually calling you are virtually zero."

"All right, I get it. Lame, I know. So tell me, what would you say?"

"Regardless of whether your next step is social in nature or just a phone call, remember you always want to put the source in an advisory role on how to best reach your potential introduction. So let's say Mr. Jones's friend is already working with someone. I'd say something along the lines of 'If he's a friend of yours, I'd be surprised if he wasn't. I'd love to take you guys to lunch and hear more about your skiing adventures. I'm sure you have some great stories! Do you think he'd open to lunch, or would it be better if I just dropped him an e-mail to introduce myself?' If Mr. Jones tells you e-mail, obviously you need the e-mail address, but you also want to ask Sam if it's all right if you tell his friend that he's a client of yours."

"That is good! I like how you asked if you could share that he was a client rather than asking if you could use his name. I always feel like asking to use their name sounds intimidating to them. That's really good."

"Years of experience, my boy," Victor replied. "Something

else to remember is you *always* want to separate the entry from the source as early in the process as possible. By that I mean you want to establish your own rapport with the entry early on so you're no longer dependent on the source for help. Once separated from the source, he's your prospect to interact with as you please without involving the source any longer. The goal should be to spend as little time as possible in that referral dance stage with the source. Do you understand?"

"Yes, sir, I do. And that's pretty smooth, I have to admit!" I was writing notes so fast my hand started to cramp. I just hoped my notes were legible enough to read because I knew what he'd just shared with me was priceless, and I doubted his specific verbiage would be in my packet. What got me the most excited, though, was that I could actually see myself *doing* this Referral Detective thing.

Everything he'd said was true. For so long I'd obsessed about referrals but had no idea how to get them effectively. Finally I had a tool that seemed like it could actually work.

If I could get just two entries a day, which didn't seem that difficult, and 80–90% dropped out, that still left me with four to eight introductions per month. I could totally live with that! And because I expected 80–90% to drop out, I didn't feel much pressure. I had a feeling of calm I'd never experienced before when I thought about referrals. This could have such huge impact on my business. My mental calculator was in overdrive.

I sunk into what had become my favorite leather chair in Victor's den and made a promise to myself to do this Referral Detective thing and not just for my usual two weeks. I wanted to see just where it could take me!

I was so deep in thought, I jumped when I heard Victor start talking again. "I'm sorry, what did you say?"

He smiled kindly and said, "I thought I'd lost you."

"No way. I was just thinking. All these years of avoiding referrals, could it really be this easy?"

"Yes, my boy. It really is. It's not rocket science. Keep in mind, any new skill will require a period of adjustment. Just remember, like anything else, consistent implementation is the key. So start with what you believe to be your best opportunities, and then work your way through all the entries you didn't eliminate. And if you're consistent, Referral Detective *will* become a primary driver of your business."

Victor was beaming, and I think I probably was too. There was a long silence as he let his last statement sink in.

He finally broke the silence with a question I wasn't expecting, "Do you do events?"

Wondering what the question had to do with Referral Detective, I answered, "Usually quarterly, why?"

"I only ask because Referral Detective can also be extremely useful in populating events."

"How so?" I asked, puzzled.

"If you ever ask attendees to bring a friend, it gives you a much more targeted approach to getting more qualified guests. It's far more effective to say to someone, 'I'm having this great event. You know you mentioned so-and-so a couple of weeks ago. Why don't you bring them along? I'd love to meet them," rather than just asking them to bring a friend. Before all your events, I strongly recommend you cross-reference your invitation list with your Referral Detective Notebook."

"That's a fantastic idea," I exclaimed. "I'll definitely be doing that! You can count on it."

"Now remember, Referral Detective is the proactive piece and just one part of my Referral System. We covered Referral Detective first because it's a much more intricate process than the conditioning components, but the conditioning components are also very important. Over time they will boost the quantity and quality of the introductions you receive with Referral Detective."

"Bring on the conditioning." I grinned.

"I think you'll like these conditioning techniques. They're much more passive in nature, require very little effort on your part, and are designed to condition your clients to know that you want and expect referrals."

"You got my attention with the 'very little effort' part." I laughed.

He ignored my comment and continued, "The first conditioning piece is what I call the Referral Process Explained component, which you should do once a year, preferably in the first quarter. You'll go through this process with all of the A, B+, and B clients you'd like to duplicate. So let me again begin with a question. What are the top three reasons you think are behind people's reluctance to give referrals?"

"I guess they're afraid I'll lose their referral's money," I answered.

"That's definitely one of the reasons, but unfortunately, that's not one you can control. Maybe you will, hopefully you won't. The second reason is that they're afraid you're going to hound the referral and that person won't appreciate them giving you their name. A third reason is that they're concerned about confidentiality issues. Both of these we can do something about. If we can eliminate two of three major objections to giving referrals before they happen, do you think that would clear the way for more referrals in your business?"

I didn't have to think long before answering, "I'm sure it would. So how do I do it?"

"Once a year when you're doing a review for someone you'd like to duplicate as a client, you take them through the Referral Process Explained. It takes just about a minute or so to do, and you'll do it at the very end of the review as a 'by the way' statement."

"Okay. So you're explaining your process to them?"

"Exactly."

"What referral process?" I asked innocently.

Victor chuckled. "So I can assume you have no referral process?"

"You assume correctly since I never got referrals, I didn't exactly have a process for them."

"Touché. But that's all about to change. So this is how it would flow. You're at the end of your review, and you say, 'By the way, there's one last item I'd like to review with you, Ms. Client. I'd like to take just a minute to go through my referral process so you're comfortable with it and you can ask any questions you may have.' This is for the client's benefit, but at the same time, it also serves as a conditioning device. It clearly tells the client in a completely nonthreatening way that you want and expect referrals."

"That's awesome! I like how you're telling them you expect referrals, but it's presented in a service kind of package. It's like it's just another agenda item to go through with them. Very cool. To them, it also probably looks like you get referrals on a regular basis. I mean after all, you have a referral process, right? Just one problem—I don't have a referral process! Actually, I'm not even sure what a referral process would look like."

"Well, let's remedy that right now, shall we? So tell me, what have you done in the past when you've gotten a referral?"

"I don't know. On those rare occasions that I have gotten one, I guess I just called them and tried to get an appointment. If they said yes, they came in. If they said no, I'd ask if I could put them on my e-newsletter list and hope they came around at some point. Maybe I'd call them once more after a couple of newsletters went out. Doesn't sound very professional, does it?"

"Finesse, my boy. You need some finesse and, of course, a system. So what do you think would look professional?"

"I'm not sure. I guess I should send them something introducing myself or something like that."

"You're definitely getting warmer," Victor encouraged. "Allow me to assist. Remember our objectives here. We want to eliminate their concern about hounding the referral and address the confidentiality issue."

I wrote the two objectives at the top of my new page. Then I scribbled "Referral Process" in big letters underneath.

"So if it were me, this is what my referral process might look like. After my 'by the way statement' to my client, I would proceed to let them know that when I receive a referral, I always get the e-mail address and phone number of the person being referred. The first thing I do is send the referral an introductory e-mail. The primary purpose of this e-mail is to let them know I'll be calling soon so they're expecting my call. In the e-mail, I share with them who referred them to me, what firm I work for, and I may include a sentence or two about my planning approach."

"So after the e-mail you'd call them, right?"

"Correct. My second step is to call them to introduce myself. I would make it perfectly clear to my client that I never hound anyone. If the referral wishes to receive additional information, I add them to my e-newsletter list. If they don't, they won't ever hear from me again."

"I get it. So you answer the hounding objective before it even comes up. Nice!"

"Then I'd tell my client that should their referral choose to take the next step, I send them my introductory kit and schedule an appointment. This is when I find out the specifics of their particular situation and determine if I can help. If we're a good fit, I begin my analysis and put together a plan for them. And of course, like every client relationship, I keep everything strictly confidential."

"And then voila." I laughed. "You've handled the confidentiality thing!"

"I would then continue by telling them that if for any reason the referral and I are not a good fit, I still provide them with a one-page recommendation sheet that I feel will position them better going forward."

I wasn't sure I understood why he would do that. "That's nice and all, but why take the time to make recommendations if they're not a good fit and they're not going to become a client?"

"Ah." Victor smiled. "By including this as part of your referral process, you let the client know in advance that you don't necessarily take every referral you get. It also serves as a goodwill gesture so your client knows, regardless of whether you take their referral, that person will leave with something of value from you. Most importantly, you avoid being put in the position of having to take referrals you don't want simply because they came from a good client."

"Brilliant!" I exclaimed. "That's happened to me a couple of times. I felt like I had to take a referral well below my minimums because it came from a good client. This is a great solution!"

"Then I would finish by asking if this is a process they feel comfortable with and ask if they have any questions. Assuming the answers to these questions are yes and no respectively, I thank them for coming in and ask them if there's anything else I can help with. I do *not* ask them for a referral. I'm strictly planting a referral seed with them through this process, which as I mentioned takes about one minute."

"I see how that could be a powerful conditioning technique," I marveled.

"So do you think you could incorporate the Referral Process Explained into your reviews with the clients you wish to duplicate?"

"Definitely. It's low-key, it nips those referral objections in the bud, and I don't have to ask for a referral. What more could I ask for? I do have one question though. What goes in the introductory kit?"

"That's up to you, my boy," he answered. "I would suggest you include a small brochure—a trifold would work quite nicely. I think the large brochures are a waste of money.

Most people don't read them. A trifold with lots of white space and bold to direct the eye to the items you wish to highlight works quite well."

"Brochures tend to be so firm-oriented. Is there something else I could put in there that's more unique to me?"

"Absolutely. You might want to include a more detailed, personalized one-pager that outlines your specific planning process and your bio. Again, lots of white space and use bold effectively. It can be front and back, and I strongly recommend that you laminate it. It's a psychological phenomenon. When something is laminated, people perceive it as having more value and therefore don't throw it away as readily. Of course, include your business card. I'd also include a brief bio on your assistant and her responsibilities. Put all of that neatly into a folder, and there's your introductory kit."

I listened carefully as I took notes. "Sounds easy enough. I'll get to work on putting together my introductory kit as soon as I get back to the office. I guess I'll start by seeing what the firm has in the way of trifolds. Wow, I'm on my way to having an actual referral system. What's next?"

Victor's expression was one of satisfaction. "Next is quite easy. Whenever you create a WOW experience for someone, I have one simple sentence I'd like you to always remember to use. And by a WOW experience, I mean a client who is delighted with something you did or repeatedly thanks you for a service you provided or says they're so happy they went forward with one of your recommendations, or an investment you suggested did particularly well. I consider all of these WOW experiences. Would you agree?"

"That about covers it for me in the WOW area, but what's the sentence?" I asked anxiously.

"First I'll give you the sentence, and then I will explain why I used the specific wording I did. The sentence is 'You probably can't think of anyone right now, but if you have friends or family who might be interested in going through a similar process, just let me know.'"

"That sounds like you're asking for a referral to me," I said suspiciously.

"Let me put your mind at ease. This is another conditioning device, and you are not asking for a referral. Rather, you are simply making a statement."

"Well, I guess that's true."

"The reason we begin by saying, 'You probably can't think of anyone right now' is because it removes the awkwardness and stress on both sides. Have we wandered too far out of your comfort zone with this one?"

I thought about it carefully and repeated the sentence a couple of times to myself to see how it felt before I answered, "Nope. I can handle it, but I can only handle it because of the 'you probably can't think of anyone right now' part."

"Fair enough. You should try to use this sentence once a day with someone. That gives you the opportunity to condition a person a day. It also encourages you to create WOW experiences." He winked.

"Okay, so we have Referral Detective, the Referral Process Explained, and the 'You probably can't think of anyone right now' sentence. What is the final piece of the system?"

"I've saved the easiest step for last," said Victor. "The last part of the system is to send a referral letter to clients once a year. Henry included a quite effective one in your packet. Again, you want to target the clients you wish to duplicate with the letter: A, B+, and B. No follow-up to the letter is required on your part. From my experience, follow-up after a referral letter adds very little in additional results. So just send it out and be done with it."

"No follow-up?"

"None required," he answered and then continued, "Expect a few referrals to trickle in, but that is not really the purpose of the letter. The purpose of the letter is to–"

"I know. It's to condition clients to think in terms of referrals and plant the seed that I want and expect them," I blurted out.

"Precisely! Also, the beauty of the referral letter is that it's not awkward for you or the client. They get the letter, and they either send you a referral or the letter ends up in the trash. No muss, no fuss as they say. It also gives you the opportunity, given the right wording, to tell the client exactly who you're looking for in a referral. That's a luxury you aren't often afforded, so take advantage of it."

Victor smiled, but I noticed for the first time since I met him, he looked tired. I glanced down at my watch and realized I'd been there for almost four hours.

He stretched his neck before stating almost victoriously, "And that, my boy, is my Referral System."

"How can I *ever* thank you for sharing this with me?" I asked.

"By using it to reach your full potential, my boy. You are not even close," he replied.

"Thank you, sir."

"The privilege was mine, Luke. Have a spectacular week," he said with a weary smile.

As if on cue, Henry appeared carrying an envelope with my packet for the week. I gathered all my papers and stuffed them in my briefcase. I looked up to tell Victor good-bye, but he was gone. It was as if he'd vanished.

Stunned by his sudden disappearance, I stumbled out of the room, following Henry to the front door.

"Uh, is he okay?" I asked, concerned. "He looked really tired today."

"Mr. Guise is fine, I can assure you, sir," he answered.

"I wanted to tell him good-bye. Where did he go? I looked up and he was gone."

Henry smiled. Ignoring the question, he opened the door and said, "I look forward to your visit next week, sir."

I paused briefly. Confused, I muttered, "Me too, Henry." The door closed gently behind me.

CHAPTER TO-DO LIST

1. Use the **12-Minute Tip** to implement changes flaw-
    lessly and consistently.

2. Use the **Referral Detective Strategy**© every single
    day.

    -   Get your **Referral Detective Notebook** — a pock-
        et-calendar-sized or checkbook-sized notebook
        with blank pages.

    -   Each entry should have the date of the conver-
        sation, the source and notes about the entry. A
        proper name is not necessary.

    -   Entries can come from anyone, not just clients.

    -   Use the **7-Second Scan**.

    -   Use **Bait Questions** to generate entries.

    -   Average two entries per day five days a week.

    -   Avoid making judgment calls on the quality of
        entries until you develop your **Referral Detec-
        tive Hit List.**

    -   Develop your Referral Detective Hit List based
        on the quality of the source and notes on the en-
        try.

    -   How you handle the next step — social vs. pure
        business — depends on your style as an advisor
        and the personality of the source.

- Always notice and take advantage of opportunities to condition your clients for referrals.

- Separate the entry from the source as early as possible.

- When holding events, always cross-reference your invitation list with your Referral Detective Notebook for possible entries to have clients bring with them.

3. Use the **Referral Process Explained** once a year, preferably in the first quarter with clients you wish to duplicate.

4. Use the "You probably can't think of anyone right now" sentence once a day to condition at least one client per day to think in terms of referrals.

5. Send a referral letter once a year to clients you wish to duplicate.

For Additional Resources, go to:

**www.executivetransformations.com/
plateau2pinnacle-additionalresources**

6. BRANDING

"You can't build a reputation on what you are going to do."

— Henry Ford

The rain came down in sheets. Lightning flashed across the dark sky so frequently, it reminded me of those obnoxious strobes Aimee and I bought for Ethan's Halloween party last year. I wondered now how he'd ever talked me into buying those crazy things.

I was exhausted and needed a break before starting the 45-minute drive up to Victor's house. Both my assistant and ops manager had been out with the flu all week, and the market was in the midst of one of its bipolar spells.

However, my success ritual was a solid habit now and one I looked forward to every morning. This week I realized what a grounding force it had become in my life. Ordinarily, I would have been totally stressed out between fielding calls from nervous clients and making sure nothing fell through the cracks with Ashley out.

I'd definitely been busy but not stressed. Victor, of course, had been right. Because I was so diligent with my client contact schedule, the phone rang a lot less, and when the market plummeted this week, I'd proactively made calls to all my A, B+, and B clients just to give them an update and reassure them. They were appreciative and felt taken care of. I felt professional and in control.

The only thing I hadn't been able to fit in was my lunch with Joe. Ever since Ben's death, I'd made it a point to have lunch with him every week or two. It killed me to do it, but with Ashley out, I had to call him and postpone. He understood, but I could tell he was disappointed. I vowed not to postpone on him again. I'd just find a way to fit it in no matter what.

As I waited in traffic, I scanned the street for some sort of sanctuary. Finally I spotted a Starbucks about a block down. I watched an SUV pull out of a parking place right in front of the door. Tapping my fingers impatiently on the steering wheel, I held my breath, hoping no one would snag it before I got there.

I slipped into the coveted spot with room to spare. As I made a dash for the door, a gust of wind yanked my umbrella inside out. By the time I stumbled through the doorway, I was drenched and irritated, the afterglow of my parking victory diminished by the clouds outside. I ordered a latte with a well-deserved double shot and flopped into a chair all the way in the back.

As I sipped my coffee, my mind drifted back to last week's session with Victor. I had no idea how old he was, not that I was a good judge of that kind of thing anyway. I just remembered how tired his eyes looked at the end of our session. His sudden and unexpected disappearance still unnerved me. It was just plain weird, and so was Henry's response, or lack of response to my questions about it.

Victor was as mysterious as he was wise, but then again, this business always attracted people who were different. Both my business and my attitude had improved dramatically in just the couple of months we'd been meeting together. Thanks to Joe, Victor had "appeared" when I needed him most.

Ding! My thoughts were interrupted by the familiar sound signaling I had a text. I looked down at my phone and was surprised to see it was from Henry. Funny, Henry didn't strike me as a big texter. I groaned as I read his message asking me to come a little early today.

Well, at least the caffeine was starting to kick in. I glanced outside, surprised. The rain had slacked to just a drizzle. Tossing my shredded umbrella into the nearest trashcan, I felt my usual Thursday anticipation beginning to build. I maneuvered my way through traffic and started up the hill to Victor's home.

The coffee did its job. I arrived and was knocking on the heavy glass door in what seemed like a blink. Henry opened it immediately.

"Good afternoon, sir. Thank you for arriving early today. Mr. Guise has some business to attend to this evening and wanted to ensure you had your full allotment of time."

"No problem, Henry." I wondered just what kind of business he was dabbling in now.

He looked past me and marveled, "You brought a double rainbow with you!"

I turned to see a bright double arc, even more vivid framed against the black sky. "Wait, Henry, let me take a picture," I said as I fumbled for my iPhone.

He looked surprised. I couldn't tell for sure but thought I detected a slight smirk on his face. I'd loved rainbows since I was a little kid. My friends had always given me a hard time about it, but Aimee thought they were romantic. "For my wife, Henry," I clarified as I snapped the picture.

"Ah, yes, sir. For your wife." His smirk turned into a smile.

Henry led me back to the den while balancing a silver

tray that held a pitcher of his highly addictive strawberry lemonade. He set it down on Victor's desk and retreated, gently shutting the door behind him.

Victor was on the phone, speaking in a foreign language I didn't recognize. He scowled as he fiddled with a Montblanc pen, his irritation unmistakable. Waving me in, he grunted with finality and abruptly tossed the phone on his desk.

He changed from cold to warm in an instant. "Well, hello, my boy! Quite the rainbow spectacular out there, wouldn't you say?"

"Yes, sir, it is."

"There's nothing like a good rainbow to give you some perspective." His voice trailed off.

There was a long pause. I watched him patiently, not sure how to respond or if I should even try. He sat down, and when he finally looked up, I could tell he was back from wherever he'd been. "So tell me. How was your week?"

"I've had better," I answered honestly. "Ashley was out, so it was one of those weeks. I was really busy, but I'm not sure I have a lot to show for it."

I replayed the week in my mind and suddenly remembered the bright spots. "But I'm happy to report that my new client contact schedule did help me navigate a difficult week, and it really paid off with one client in particular."

"How so?" he asked.

"Well, you know I have to call some C clients every day to get all the calls in. I got to this one guy on the list who was always a real pain. You know the type. He complained about everything, never took my advice, and then wanted me to discount for him."

Victor leaned back in his chair and nodded. I couldn't imagine Victor ever having to deal with that kind of client, but if he'd been a financial advisor, I knew he had.

"I was all ready to fire him as a client on the call and get rid of another one of those nonproductive C clients. But then his wife, Rebecca, answered." I paused for effect and then continued, "Turns out, she divorced him! She was so glad I called because she'd just received a $500,000 check from the divorce. She's a nice lady and is coming in tomorrow to open an account in her name, and guess what she's bringing with her? The $500,000 check she's depositing with me."

"Excellent, my boy! And you said you didn't have a lot to show for your week." He chuckled.

"And I did send your referral letter off to Compliance for approval. Since I've never done anything proactive when it comes to referrals, I thought the letter might be the best way to introduce my clients to the whole referral idea. You know — in a nonthreatening way."

"Ah, and perhaps get you used to the whole proactive concept as well — in a nonthreatening way, of course."

"Well, yes, there's that too," I admitted. Nothing got past Victor. I should have known better than to even try.

"I thought I'd wait until the first quarter to do the Referral Process Explained, since that's just a couple of months away. That's what you suggested anyway, right?"

"Correct," he answered. "If we weren't so close to the end of the year, I'd have you integrate it into your review process immediately. However, because you're sending out the referral letter in the next couple of weeks, following up with the Referral Process Explained in the first quarter should be excellent timing. And what about Referral Detective? How did you do there?"

"Okay — but not great. I had trouble remembering, even though the Referral Detective Notebook was right next to my phone. I realized if I could remember to consciously ask the bait questions, I tended to remember the 7-Second Scan as well. But if I didn't remember the bait questions, I usually forgot the 7-Second Scan too."

"Good observation! So how many entries did you get this week?"

I fidgeted and finally answered reluctantly, "I only got five."

My lack of productivity didn't seem to faze Victor in the slightest. He smiled and for a split second seemed almost grandfatherly. I wondered if he had kids, grandkids, all that. He really surprised me with his Labrador retriever confession a couple of weeks ago, so I guessed anything was possible. One week he's having helicopters pick him up, the next week he's ordering pizza, and then he just disappears. Having Victor for a grandfather would be interesting, that's for sure.

"That's five potential introductions you wouldn't have had otherwise. Referral Detective is simple but not always as easy as it sounds. The important thing is to begin forming the habit so it's part of who you are and what you do every day. If you can do that, even when you have a challenging week, you'll never come away empty handed.

"I'm determined to get 10 next week no matter what," I announced.

"Eventually, we want Referral Detective to be something you do without even thinking, regardless of what's happening in the markets, your office, or your personal life. Always remember, forming any new habit, especially a good one, requires only two things from you — persistence and time. Since you seemed to have linked the bait questions with the 7-Second Scan, what will you use as a cue to remember to use both next week?"

"Well, I have the book right next to my phone, and that has helped me remember, but not every time. I've tried using sticky notes in the past to remind me of stuff, but it doesn't take me long to start ignoring those too."

I tried to think of something that would help me remember. Then I had a sudden flash of inspiration. "I've got it! I'll have my kids make me a sign that says 'Bait Questions & 7-Second Scan.' They'll make something I can't forget!"

"Bold colors, with sparkles and glitter I'm sure." Victor

laughed. "Excellent idea. The artwork of children is always unforgettable! Perhaps you should also have them create one to help you remember the 'you probably can't think of anyone right now' phrase you use when you have those WOW moments we discussed last week."

"That's something I know I'm going to need help remembering." I made a note to ask the kids to create something "unforgettable" for me. "So what's on tap for today?"

Victor's eyes twinkled. "It's something you hear a lot about in the industry, and it's something every advisor would like to have in his or her business but very few do. Care to venture a guess?"

"I have no idea. That could be a lot of things."

"Very true. Let me give you a few more hints. 'Fifteen minutes can save you 15% or more on car insurance.' Or try this. Envision a wide green line on the ground that leads people directly to your office. Or perhaps consider a price gun that lets people decide what they want to pay for your services. Any ideas now?"

I carefully considered his examples. Unsure, I answered, "Advertising?"

"Close but not exactly. Today, we're going to talk about branding. A strong company brand is helpful, but it does very little to set the individual advisor apart from others within the industry or even within the same firm. It's the personal brand, not the company brand that ultimately leads to more assets, referrals, and revenue."

"That's probably true," I replied, "but how do you develop a personal brand with Compliance looking over your shoulder all the time? I think they would frown on advisors developing their own personal brand."

"Good point. The answer to that, my boy, is the old good news/bad news scenario. The bad news is, as Compliance oversight and regulations become ever more stringent, the individual advisor is limited in what he or she can do to build their brand. The good news is there are a couple of very powerful and effective ways an advisor can build a personal brand within the confines of Compliance. That's precisely what we're going to talk about today."

I pulled out my notebook and my trusty Victor pen. He was right. This was one of those subjects that the firm, as well as wholesalers, always stressed as important. The only problem was no one ever gave you any suggestions on how exactly to do it. I knew that would change today.

Victor waited until I got settled and then began in his scholarly tone, "Branding, like referrals, begins and ends with conditioning. Anyone can have a brand, but it takes a conscious and continual effort to build a successful one. It is not a task that you do once and then you're done. It's something that you are consistently building all the time in everything you do. The things you say, the things you write, and the person you are every day, all reinforce your brand. For better or worse, I might add."

The subject of branding always intrigued me yet seemed so out of reach. I was eager to learn more and asked, "How do you even begin to narrow down and define what you want your brand to be or say about you? I mean, we wear a lot of different hats."

"Ah, for many advisors there lies the challenge," he acknowledged. "What do you do for a living?"

That was a question I should have expected but didn't. Unfortunately, I lacked a brilliant comeback, so I muttered the standard "I'm a financial advisor with Strong Hauser."

Ignoring my lack of imagination, he continued, "Believe it or not, crafting a powerful elevator speech is a great place to start defining your brand. The process gives you clarity. It forces you to consider exactly what it is that you wish to convey to others. In fact, this is where successful branding begins. Although most advisors recognize the importance of having a strong elevator speech, most would admit that theirs could use some work."

"I know mine certainly could!"

"There is a very real distinction to be made between a *powerful elevator speech* and all the other ones out there. By powerful, I do not mean a long dissertation about 'building wealth for high net-worth investors coupled with the legacy planning necessary to set up proper vehicles for effectively passing wealth to the next generation in the most tax-efficient manner.' Nor am I a proponent of the old standby that you just used. Neither represents anything significant to anyone. For an elevator speech to be truly powerful, it must meet six very specific criteria."

I leaned forward and turned the page in my notebook with such anticipation, I almost ripped it in the process. Victor stared, obviously amused. I could feel my face flush. I took a deep breath and smiled. "I'm ready."

"Very well then. First and foremost, a powerful elevator speech must be very short—absolutely no more than one sentence in length. Consider your elevator speech the hook. You have seconds to capture a potential prospect's attention and keep it. So you must make every word count. This is your one and only opportunity to make a first impression."

"So how do you hook them in one sentence?"

"In order to be a successful hook, your elevator speech should be somewhat mysterious. Though it may seem counterintuitive, the person you're talking to should be a little unsure of exactly what you do, which brings us to the second criterion. Your elevator speech should always spark questions. You're off to a great start with a new prospect when you're able to hook them into asking questions. Would you agree?"

"Sure, but usually as soon as they find out you're a financial advisor, a lot of times they run, not walk the other way!"

Victor laughed. "Oh, I remember those days well."

"I understand it should be short and that you want them to ask questions," I said. "But I have no idea how you would make an elevator speech mysterious."

"You'll see what I mean in a minute when I give you some examples, but let me move on to criterion #3 which is, you must have two or three strong follow-up points that clarify your process. The last thing you want is to successfully hook them, only to start rambling and lose them once they begin asking questions. Think in terms of bullet points. You don't want to go into great detail. The goal is to leave them wanting more."

I had to admit, this seemed a little beyond my capabilities, so I confessed, "I understand what you're saying, but I'm not exactly the most creative guy in the world. It seems to me you'd almost have to be a master wordsmith to do what you're talking about here."

"Not really," he answered. "What do you want people to most remember about you? What makes you different? Why should they do business with you over every other advisor out there? These are the questions you should ask yourself as you're developing your follow-up points. Once you have the basic theme, you can begin to whittle it down to short and concise bullet points."

"When you put it like that, it doesn't sound all that difficult I guess. So what's the fourth criteria?"

"Ah, the fourth criterion is the essence of what makes an elevator speech powerful. It should prompt prospects to question their own situation. Their immediate response should be to wonder if they currently have or don't have what you stated in your elevator speech. Above all else, you want them to leave with a seed planted that they may actually need you."

I just stared at him. "How could you ever accomplish all that with a one-sentence elevator speech? I'm going to need some examples real soon," I said, unconvinced it was even possible.

"Patience, my boy. Patience! The fifth and one of the most important components of your elevator speech is that it must be something you feel comfortable articulating to others. Keep in mind that anything new is going to feel awkward at first. So you must practice until it feels natural. The best elevator speech in the world does you absolutely no good if you don't use it. I suggest you say it aloud to yourself every morning in the mirror while shaving. Practice using different intonations and emphasizing different words. Pay attention to the expression on your face as you're saying it. Practice it until it rolls off the tongue as easily as stating your name. Remember, this is the only opportunity you have to make a first impression, so make it memorable!"

"Are we at the examples part yet?" I asked.

"You have arrived." He chuckled. "Here are some examples of powerful elevator speeches that all meet the above criteria:

'I deal with people who are sick and tired of the usual piecemeal approach to retirement.'

'I determine and analyze people's retirement number.'

'I identify where portfolios are vulnerable.'

'I help people secure and protect their paycheck in retirement.'"

"Hmm, those are a lot different than any elevator speech I've ever heard. You don't even say what firm you're with?"

"No," he answered. "Is that really necessary in your elevator speech? Don't you plan on giving them a business card anyway?"

"I guess that's true," I said.

Victor sensed my skepticism. Undaunted, he continued, "Most people are used to hearing the exact elevator speech you gave me when I asked you what you did for a living. Eliminating the name of your firm in your initial elevator speech is in itself unusual and adds that element of mystery."

"I don't know about this. You didn't even say you were a financial advisor in your examples. How exactly is that going to work?" I asked.

"Your occupation and firm will emerge soon enough," he answered. Either the prospect will ask, or it will become apparent when you hand them your business card. Remember, the whole point is to get them asking questions."

What he said made a lot of sense, and the examples he gave *were* compelling. I guess the real question revolved around criteria #5. Could I make the shift from my worn-out but comfortable "I'm-a-financial-advisor-with" elevator speech to what he proposed here? Everything he'd taught me so far had been right on, but this most definitely involved moving out of my comfort zone.

"I believe it was Neale Donald Walsch who said, 'Life begins at the end of your comfort zone.'" He smiled and then added, "You, my boy, have just reached the end of yours."

I stared at him in disbelief. "How do you do that?"

"Do what?" he asked, feigning innocence.

"Read my mind! That's what, and it's not the first time either," I answered a little too loudly.

"How could I miss it?" he asked calmly. "It's written all over your face."

"Geez, am I that transparent?" I asked. I could feel my face turning scarlet.

"Most people don't pay very close attention, Luke, so I think you'll be just fine."

Anxious to change the subject, I said, "So you were talking earlier about the elevator speech making them question their own situation and planting the seed that they may need you. I like the way that sounded. Can you expand on that a little bit?"

"It is human nature to process almost everything we see or hear through the 'how does that affect me' lens. Take advantage of this universal human trait with your elevator speech. In each of my examples, notice how the prospect is led to question their current situation.

I wonder if *I* have a piecemeal approach to retirement.

I wonder what *my* retirement number is.

I wonder if *my* portfolio is vulnerable.

I wonder what *my* paycheck will be in retirement.

"When your elevator speech causes prospects to question their current situation, it has accomplished a very important objective. Your follow-up points should reinforce in their mind that they need you. Be clear and phrase every bullet point as succinctly as possible."

"So really the whole point of a powerful elevator speech and the follow-up points is to get the prospect engaged, asking questions, and plant the seed in their mind that they may just need you," I thought out loud.

"Exactly. When the prospect is asking questions, they're interested, and when they're interested, you've taken the first step in moving them from prospect to client."

"I guess I never put that much thought into an elevator speech before. I mean I never thought of it in terms of having such specific objectives."

"Most advisors don't, and that leads me to the last component of a powerful elevator speech. You should always end your conversation with a hot-button question. This is a question that provides you with a reason to contact the prospect in the future."

"You mean like do you have a financial plan or something like that?"

"Again, you're close, my boy. What are the two most powerful motivators when it comes to the markets?"

Without even thinking, I responded, "Fear and greed."

"Exactly," Victor exclaimed. "You want to tap into one of those two emotions with your hot-button question. In my experience, fear is usually the stronger of the two. Although everyone knows they should have some sort of plan, I'm not sure that it's a strong enough hot-button question. The plan question is more likely to elicit feelings of guilt than actual fear. A more appropriate hot-button question would be something like 'So what are you most concerned with in your portfolio right now?' By including the 'right now,' you've created some sense of urgency as well. Do you see how that's a stronger hot-button question than asking about their plan?"

"Yes, sir, I do," I answered. "But what if they say, 'I'm pretty happy right now'?"

"Good question because you're likely to get that response on more than one occasion. If that's their answer, I'd respond by saying something like 'Well, that's good. The markets, in general, *have* been kind lately. Let's keep in touch, though, and when you have a concern, just give me a call. I'll check it out for you.' Just like referrals, the calmer and more casual you are, the more at ease the prospect will be."

"Transference, right?"

"Precisely," he said. "The key to the hot-button question is to remain calm and casual regardless of their response."

"Well, I know what I'll be doing this week," I said with a smile. "I'm going to be working on a new elevator speech. Mind if I borrow one of yours?"

Victor nodded. "Imitation *is* the highest form of flattery! So by all means, use what you think will work for you. Remember, one of the most important aspects of your new elevator speech is that you're confident enough that you'll actually use it and not revert back to what feels comfortable. Once you decide on one, you must practice, practice, practice!"

"Got it," I answered. There was no denying that my old elevator speech had accomplished absolutely nothing. I'd been pretty skeptical at first, but the idea of developing one that could possibly plant a seed with the prospect that they might need me was pretty appealing. "I do have one question. Developing this new elevator speech is great and all, but what exactly does it have to do with branding?"

"The elevator speech gives you clarity on what exactly you want to convey to people – prospects and clients alike. You condensed that theme down to a single sentence. Now we're going to condense it down even further to its least common denominator – a few words that will serve as your primary conditioning phrase."

"You know what my next question is going to be, right?" I laughed.

Always quick to read my mind, he said as casually as he could, "A primary conditioning phrase is your very own '15 minutes can save you 15% or more on car insurance.' Say that to anyone, and immediately they have visions of Geico dancing in their heads. As unlikely as it may seem, this is an example of one of the most successful conditioning phrases in recent history."

"And it's not like it's a catchy phrase or anything. It's the lizard that made it stick," I commented.

"Gecko, I believe," said Victor.

"What?"

"I believe the lizard you're referring is actually a gecko." He smiled, obviously amused. "In any case, your primary conditioning phrase *is* your brand. Developing it involves carefully considering exactly what you want people to most remember about you. This is precisely why we'll borrow it from your elevator speech."

"If the elevator speech is a single sentence, what can you possibly borrow from it? Aren't the conditioning phrase and the elevator speech kind of the same thing?"

"Not exactly. Your conditioning phrase is just that – a phrase. It's not a complete sentence, but rather a few key words that you can easily build a sentence around and use in a variety of ways as part of your daily communication. Do you understand?"

"I think so." I said as I scratched notes furiously in my

notebook. I hoped I could read this stuff. Last week's notes had been a challenge to decipher.

Victor continued, "You'll use your primary conditioning phrase in everything you do—every conversation, every meeting, and every piece of correspondence. The phrase should be included as 'a tagline in your e-mail signature and on the bottom of all correspondence that leaves your office on letterhead. If you write handwritten notes, take your stationary or notecards to a printer and have your conditioning phrase professionally printed at the bottom."

"Okay, I get the point of a powerful elevator speech. And I get that you want clients to remember it and connect you with the phrase, but what does that do for you exactly?"

"You want clients to remember it and be able to communicate it to others. Those 'others' are your potential referrals. You see, not only do we want to condition clients to think in terms of referrals, but we also want them to communicate the right message to potential referrals. If you consistently use the same phrase, that's the phrase they'll remember and repeat."

"I think it's time for another example." I gulped down some of the strawberry lemonade Henry had left for us.

"Very well. Which of the elevator speeches I shared with you would you like to use as an example?"

"Uhh. I liked the one about identifying your retirement number."

"In that case, your conditioning phrase is obviously 'retirement number.' You can use that phrase in a multitude of ways. For example:

'I believe everyone should know their *retirement number* so they can plan for it.'

'The sooner we identify your *retirement number*, the sooner we can start planning for it.'

'You're already ahead of most investors who have no idea what their *retirement number* is.'

'Do you think your children know their *retirement numbers?*'

"Your e-mail tagline could be something like 'Planning for your retirement number today and moving towards your dreams for tomorrow.'"

"I get it now," I said, nodding triumphantly. "I guess your conditioning phrase is only a few words because that's all people can really remember, right?"

"Exactly," said Victor. "Now envision this scenario. Your best client is talking to his friends, and the subject of investments comes up. His friends start talking about how their advisor put them in this stock or that bond, and your client asks rather smugly, 'That's great, but do you know your retirement number? That's the first thing *my* advisor did for me!'"

"Whoa, that is powerful!"

"That's precisely what we want your conditioning phrase and your brand to do for you. Remember, the strength of your brand depends upon the strength of your conditioning, and that is purely a function of repetition. "

"This is awesome! I can't wait to start working on my elevator speech and my conditioning phrase. I like the way everything you've taught me all works together — the client contact schedule, the referral process, and now the branding. It's got to make a huge difference in my business."

"I'm sure it will. Successful branding is not rocket science, but it can make a stellar difference in your business. Just as the key to real estate is location, location, location; the key to branding is repetition, repetition, repetition. Remember that, my boy!"

"And it doesn't require a lot of extra time, work, or money. You have to like that!"

"That's true," said Victor. "It does, however, require conscious consideration of the words you want to brand in the minds of your clients and prospects, as well as the discipline to use those words consistently.

"Use every opportunity as a conditioning opportunity to build your brand, and your business will grow, my boy. It will grow."

"Thank you," I murmured.

I studied Victor as he stood. We were obviously done with today's session. He had an air of power about him even staring out the window. I followed his gaze, trying to figure out what had captured his attention so completely.

Wisps of leftover storm clouds hung like a tattered shade, halfheartedly blocking the setting sun. The violet and pink tie-dyed sky cast an odd lighting over the whole room. Victor seemed to glow as if he had a strange aura outlining his entire body.

"The privilege was mine, Luke," he said finally. "Use your new knowledge well."

"I will. Uh, I'll see you next Thursday?"

"I wouldn't miss it."

I noticed Henry standing quietly behind my chair, packet in hand. I stuffed my notebook in my briefcase and glanced up quickly, fully expecting Victor to be gone. He stood behind his desk now, but the strange aura was still there, brighter than before.

I followed Henry out of the door, resisting the strong urge to look back one more time.

CHAPTER TO-DO LIST

1. Develop a powerful elevator speech using the six criteria outlined in the chapter.

    *   Start with one sentence that serves as the hook. It should be mysterious enough to spark questions.

    *   It should have two or three short, concise bullet points to clarify your process.

        ➢ What do you want them to most remember about you?

        ➢ What makes you unique?

    *   It should make prospects question their own situation and plant a seed that they may need you.

    *   You must practice it every day while shaving or putting on your makeup. Use different intonations and try emphasizing different words. Practice until it's as comfortable as saying your name.

    *   End with a hot-button question that gives you a reason to contact the prospect in the future. Always remain calm and casual regardless of their answer.

2. Develop your primary conditioning phrase from your elevator speech.

    *   Include your primary conditioning phrase in a tagline in your e-mail signature.

- Use your primary conditioning phrase in everything you do—every conversation, every meeting, and every piece of correspondence.

- If you write handwritten notes, take your stationery or notecards to a printer and have your conditioning phrase professionally printed at the bottom.

For Additional Resources, go to:

**www.executivetransformations.com/
plateau2pinnacle-additionalresources**

7. THE POWER OF THE PLAN

*"Do the right thing. It will gratify some people
and astonish the rest."*

– Mark Twain

I was feeling great. I'd had one of those rare weeks where
everything fell perfectly into place. I'd started using my new
conditioning phrase in everything I did just like Victor said.
And the bullet points I developed for my elevator speech just
may have helped me close my first Referral Detective entry.

A couple of days after Victor first introduced me to
Referral Detective, Joe and I were having lunch together
when he mentioned a good friend of his who'd just sold
a small tugboat business. Naturally I'd forgotten my
Referral Detective notebook, so I immediately put the
entry in my phone. That seemed to work better for me than
the notebook because my phone was always with me. Joe
agreed to contact the guy and talked him into coming to
see me.

It had taken several meetings, but yesterday, I had used
my conditioning phrase and reinforced it with my bullet

points. The whole branding thing gave me the clarity I needed to articulate exactly how and why I was different from the other two advisors he'd been considering. You never know for sure why someone decides to go with you, but the branding work I'd done gave me a new confidence I'd never felt before. Not only did he decide to go with me, but he was moving $3,000,000, mostly in cash!

Now I just had to figure out what to do with the money. I wanted to do the very best job I could for him, so I definitely had some work ahead of me. I wasn't complaining though. It was a good problem to have. Today, arriving at Victor's, *I* was the one with the glowing aura. I laughed as I bounded up the stairs, taking two steps at time.

When I looked up, there was Henry waiting at the door for me. "Well, good afternoon, sir. You're looking quite chipper today."

"I feel chipper, Henry," I proclaimed. "I've had a fantastic week!"

"Well then, congratulations are in order." He smiled and bowed an exaggerated bow.

"Thank you, sir. And how is the old man today?" I asked.

"Mr. Guise is quite well and is awaiting your presence in the den."

As we walked together down the familiar hallway, I realized I'd never asked Henry anything about Victor or himself. He was obviously several years older than Victor. The whole aura thing had left me even more curious about them both. I didn't expect to get much out of Henry, but I decided to give it a shot.

I stopped suddenly and asked, "Henry, how long have you known Mr. Guise?"

"Oh, a long time, sir. I think it's been almost 40 years now," he answered and continued walking.

I caught up to him at the den door. "How did you guys meet?" I persisted.

He turned around to face me. "Fate." He winked and opened the door.

"Come in, my boy. How are you?" Victor boomed from across the room.

I walked in and shook his hand. "I'm uh, good, sir. Thank you," I said slowly. Still trying to process Henry's answer, I turned, but he was already gone, the door closed.

"Have a seat and tell me about your week," he said. I looked at him closely as I took my usual spot in front of the window. No aura today. I started to wonder if I'd imagined the whole thing.

I took a deep breath and told him all about my week — the branding, my conditioning phrase, my new client — every detail. When I was done, he smiled and looked like I pictured myself looking the day Ethan hit his home run in Little League.

He didn't say it, but I could tell he was proud of me. "You're coming along, my boy. You're coming along" was all he said.

"My only problem now is figuring out the best way to invest the money. I don't want to make any mistakes."

"Perfect," he beamed.

"Yes, sir, it was perfect but now..."

"No, no. I mean this is perfect timing for what we're going to discuss today!"

"Oh. What's on the agenda?"

"The power of the plan," he announced.

"You mean financial planning?" I asked. I'd learned not to assume anything when I was with Victor.

"Precisely. Do you do it?"

"Kind of informally, I guess. I have a good discovery process I think. Once I go through that with a client and get a handle on their risk tolerance and their primary investment objectives, then I decide how the money should be allocated. The firm has different fee-based models based on risk tolerance. I forget how many they have, but most of my clients end up in their moderate or moderately aggressive models. Then they get automatically rebalanced when something changes."

"That's all fine and well, but you're only talking about the investment piece. I'm talking about real, comprehensive financial planning," he said a little impatiently.

"If you're talking about doing a formal financial plan, then no, I don't do them. I'll do Monte Carlo simulations for clients. All they're really interested in anyway is if they'll have enough money to retire. I know the firm is big on financial plans, but you end up with this massive 80-page document. The client takes one look at it and starts to glaze over. To be honest, I think they're cumbersome for the client and the advisor and kind of a waste of time," I answered defiantly.

"I see. And how many of these cumbersome plans have you actually completed?" Victor asked.

I shrugged. "I don't know. Two or three maybe."

"Hmm," he said. "So based on a sample size of, let's see, two or three, you've decided that they're cumbersome for all parties involved, their value does not justify the time, and clients automatically glaze over upon seeing the document. Is that correct?"

"Look, I know they're the hot thing right now. A lot of advisors pay a lot of lip service to them, but very few actually do them on a consistent basis. And if they do, they present them and maybe revisit them once or twice if that." I could feel myself getting defensive.

"You didn't answer my question, Luke," Victor said sternly. "Based on a sample size of two or three, you feel they're cumbersome, they're not worth the time, and clients immediately glaze over when the document is placed in front of them. Is that what you're saying?"

I sighed heavily. "Yes, that's what I'm saying."

"How bonded are your clients to you?" he asked.

"They're very bonded to me, especially now that my client service model is in place."

"I'm sure they are. But how bonded would they be if another advisor did a comprehensive financial plan for them and presented it to them in bite-sized pieces they could understand and focus on? Furthermore, what if this advisor reviewed not just their investments but their complete financial picture and advised them on insurance, their mortgage, their 401K, when to take Social Security, and also reviewed how their beneficiaries were set up? And how bonded would they be if this same advisor discovered where all their assets were and proposed consolidating them under the plan? How bonded do you think they'd be in that scenario?"

Well, when he put it like that..."Probably not very," I mumbled under my breath.

"Excuse me?" he asked. "I didn't hear you."

"Not very, okay," I answered irritated, my great mood gone.

His expression softened. "Luke, being a great investment advisor or even an expert at asset allocation is no longer enough. Times have changed. The vast majority of the public still has not recovered psychologically or emotionally from 2008. They want a process, one they can see, understand, and watch unfold. Don't you want to set yourself apart from all the other advisors out there trying to sell the same products to the same people?"

"Yes, sir, I do," I conceded.

"You yourself said that advisors pay a lot of lip service to planning, but very few actually do it consistently, and if they do, they don't always do it well, correct?"

"Yes, sir."

"Well, to me that says the advisor who does financial planning well, presents it well, reviews it on a regular basis, and adjusts it as the client's life changes has a distinct competitive advantage. Would you agree?"

"Yes, sir," I answered, feeling defeated. "I know you're right. It's just that I'm comfortable with my process the way it is. The old dog new tricks thing. What you're talking about is *completely* revamping how I've done things for the last 10 years. It's going to take a lot of effort."

Victor burst into laughter. "Surely you jest! You're a bit young to be an old dog, don't you think? And relative to the massive effort you seem to feel this undertaking will require, everything you've done thus far has taken substantial effort on your part, would you agree?"

"I guess that's true," I sighed.

"Do you want to live and die by performance Luke?"

"No, sir."

"Of course you don't—especially with markets and the world as volatile as they are today! What you will find," he said slowly, "is that once you do a plan for a client and revisit it in every review you do with them, their focus begins to shift. They become considerably less interested in how their accounts are performing and much more concerned about where they stand relative to their plan. Isn't that a better way to live?"

"That would be a lot less stressful," I admitted.

"I've been hard on you today because this is very important, my boy. The window of opportunity to set yourself apart from the masses is now.

"Clients *need* you to do this for them, and they need you to do it well. It's best for them and it's best for you. You'll be providing an unsurpassed level of service, and they'll appreciate you for it. In addition to that, when you do the plan, you discover where all the assets are. And when they see that you *do* have a plan and a process, your assets and referrals will both increase."

"If you build it, they will come, huh?"

"Exactly. So to quote another classic, have I made you an offer you can't refuse?"

I smiled for the first time since I'd entered the den. "Yes, sir, you have. Just tell me what I need to do."

"Excellent. Let's begin with your discovery process. You said you have a good one. Tell me about it."

"Well, I ask clients to bring in all their statements. Sometimes they do, but they almost always forget something."

"Do you send them a letter or e-mail prior to your appointment listing everything they need to bring with them?" he asked.

"No. I usually just send one afterwards reminding them of what I still need."

"Let's try the proactive rather than reactive approach going forward, shall we? Henry has an excellent letter in your packet today with a listing of all the documents you will likely need to do a financial plan. Feel free to modify the list as you see fit."

"That makes sense. Thank you," I said, wondering how Henry knew what to put in my packet every week.

"Do you spend any time on subjective questioning during your discovery process?"

"You mean like what do they want to do in retirement?"

"Yes, exactly," he answered.

"Well, I ask them that, and I ask them when they want to retire." I opened my briefcase and pulled out my well-worn notebook and Victor pen. I instinctually knew it was time for notes.

"Don't shortchange the subjective," said Victor. "It's one of the most important areas of questioning you'll do. I'd ask them questions like: What's on their retirement bucket list? What parts of their retirement are nonnegotiable? What do they anticipate adding and giving up in retirement? What do they envision in retirement? These are all questions they have probably never been asked before. And don't be surprised if you occasionally get a married couple who have totally different ideas about retirement."

"Really?" I found that kind of hard to believe. "I always assumed couples have talked about their retirement pretty much their whole life and especially before they come to see me."

"Not necessarily," said Victor. For many people, retirement is an event in the distant future that they work toward but never give much thought to the reality of it. Ask your subjective questions first. They provide you with valuable insight.

"For instance, it's important to discover what parts of their retirement are nonnegotiable. Say for instance, visiting their grandchildren twice a year is nonnegotiable. You run your numbers, and maybe they don't have quite enough money. You know visiting the grandchildren is not something you want to cut."

"Hmm, that's pretty smart. Do you have a list of subjective questions I should be asking?"

"Henry has a list in your packet."

"I should have known that." I smiled.

"You must realize, Luke, that for most people retirement is the most dramatic transition of their life *and* it's for the rest of their life. It's bigger than getting married or even having children. And it's not just a financial transition; it's an emotional one as well."

I thought carefully about what he'd just said. "Wow. All I ever focused on was the financial transition. It's almost embarrassing that I've been in the business for 10 years and never once considered what my clients might be going through emotionally when they retired. I need to be more sensitive to that!"

"I guarantee *that* will set you apart!"

"Hmm. I can see how important the subjective questioning really is now."

Victor continued, "Another reason you want to ask your subjective questions first is to get them talking. It helps to build your bond with the client. Also, once you get them talking about their hopes, dreams, and fears in retirement, they're much more likely to provide you with complete information when you get to the financial questions."

"That makes a lot of sense. I thought I had a good discovery process, but it obviously wasn't as good as I thought it was. Thanks for forcing me into this," I teased.

Victor smiled. "Did I force you? I wasn't aware that I had," he said as innocently as he could.

I laughed. "Yes, sir, you kind of did. I was a pretty hard nut to crack when we started today."

"Oh, I've had tougher, my boy. I've had tougher."

I didn't doubt that. I thought about Victor a lot. He was so different from anyone I'd ever met. Who was he really? What had he seen in his life? I knew he'd been married at some point. Did he have kids? Where was he even from? He had the slightest hint of an accent, but I couldn't place it. What was he like when he wasn't all business, or was he all business all the time? I bet Henry knew. Maybe he was the only one who did.

"Luke?"

I jumped. "Oh, sorry, sir."

"You wandered off on me," he said.

"I'm back." I smiled.

"Well then, let's get to the glazing-over phase of the process. That would be your presentation. We've established your discovery process as different from most advisors out there. Now we want to do the same with your presentation process."

"So how exactly am I supposed to take an 80-page document and present it in a way that doesn't put the client to sleep but also covers what I need to cover?"

"That's easy," he replied. "You're going to modulize it."

"I'm not sure I understand."

"Let me explain. You said clients are most interested in

the Monte Carlo simulation and determining whether or not they're going to have enough to retire, correct?"

"Right," I answered.

"If that's what they're most concerned with, then that's what you present in your first appointment after running the plan. Then you give it to them and explain that a tremendous amount of information is covered in the plan. However, there are certain areas that are absolutely essential to a comprehensive financial planning process and you will cover each of them in the years leading up to retirement. Explain that you are going to break these areas into modules that you will discuss with them over time."

"That should have them breathing a sigh of relief," I commented.

"Indeed."

"Should I give them some kind of list of the modules I plan to cover?"

"Now you're thinking, my boy. Besides an investment module, what do you think are the key areas that should be covered with almost every client if your objective is to give them a comprehensive financial or retirement planning experience?"

I considered his question. "Well, I'd say I should probably cover a lot of the same areas as that financial advisor who's going to steal all my accounts would cover. You know the guy you mentioned earlier?"

"I remember him well." Victor smiled.

"So I guess that would mean Social Security, health care, insurance, beneficiaries, mortgage and lending, legacy planning, and a comprehensive retirement review of their pension, 401K, and IRA accounts together. Did I leave anything out?"

"That about covers it," said Victor. "The only area you might want to add is a retirement income planning module where you outline exactly where the client's income is going to come from in retirement and the order in which you'll take it from various sources."

"That makes sense for someone approaching retirement, but I have a lot clients who are already retired. What kind of planning should I do for them?"

"Excellent question! A lot of retirees feel once they're retired, their planning is done. Nothing could be further from the truth. Financial planning is even more important for retirees because usually the amount of assets they're dealing with is fixed and must last them the rest of their lives. However, with the exception of Social Security, many of the same modules will still apply. And depending on what decisions previously have or have not been made, you still may be able to advise them on Social Security as well."

"That's true but maybe with an extra emphasis on the income planning module."

"Exactly," said Victor. "Once you figure out which modules you'll want to cover with your clients, make a list of them along with a brief explanation of each and submit it to Compliance for review. Once approved, you should use this as a master document. Laminate it and give it to clients at the first planning meeting."

"Okay, so I get we're breaking down the financial planning presentation into modules, and I know which modules I'm going to use, but how exactly does the whole thing work?" I asked.

"We've already discussed how modulizing your process takes what's potentially overwhelming to the client and breaks it down into bite-sized, digestible pieces that the client can focus on and understand. It also forces a structure on you that facilitates meaningful conversations with clients on an ongoing basis," he explained.

He paused when he saw me writing furiously. Since this whole planning thing was new to me, I was frantically trying to take down every word he said. My hand was starting to cramp, so I stretched it several times before continuing.

"Ready?" he asked.

"Ready," I answered.

"You'll find that clients enjoy working through a process rather than trying to grasp what, at many times, can seem like a random approach to their finances. They see the process unfold over time, and it makes sense to them. It also gives you an opportunity to WOW them on a regular basis, and with every WOW comes an increased probability of referrals and additional assets!"

"Watch out! You're starting to make a believer out of me." I laughed. "So how often do I take them through a module?"

"That's entirely up to you and is dependent on where the client is relative to their retirement date or if they're already retired. If time or circumstances are not an immediate concern, a general rule of thumb would be one or two modules per year."

"So if I do semiannual reviews, one would be an actual module and the other would be a regular account review?"

"Remember, you want to steer them away from a performance focus and to a plan focus. So depending on what's happening in their life and in the markets, some years both reviews may cover modules with performance always taking a backseat to the plan. Other times, one may be a module and the other a pure plan review."

"And that really works? Clients really get more focused on the plan than performance?"

"Clients follow your lead. Whatever you choose to focus on is where their focus will be also."

"Hmm. I guess I'm going to have to trust you on this one. At least in the beginning."

"Fair enough," he replied.

"So how do I approach a client I've had for a long time that I probably should have done a plan for before now? How do I make a case for doing a plan at this particular point in time?"

"There are any number of ways to handle that. I think I'd explain it in much the same way as I explained it to you. 'Times have changed and the markets have changed. There is volatility all around the world. In the past we did some informal planning and focused on the investment side of the equation. However, in light of everything happening around the world, it's time we did a formal, more comprehensive financial plan. We want to ensure we've covered all the bases because real financial planning is about much more than just your investments."

"Wow, where do I sign up?"

Victor continued, "Also, because formal financial planning is new to you, it might be wise to begin targeting your B tier and work your way up as you grow comfortable with the process. After all, you have that 'old dog' mentality to contend with."

I laughed. "Good idea. I have a question. How do I keep track of where everyone is in the system and what module they're on?"

"That calls for a spreadsheet. You should have a separate spreadsheet for each client and attach it to their client record. A basic spreadsheet should have a column for each module. When you complete a module, add the date it was completed and include a place to add notes."

"Don't tell me...Henry has a sample one in my packet?"

"Indeed he does."

"I never thought I'd say it, but I like this system," I admitted. "It seems like a win-win for everybody. It's good for the client, and I like the idea of knowing where all the assets are."

"Building deep and powerful relationships is essential to the type of growth you're after, would you agree?"

"Yes, sir, I would," I answered enthusiastically.

"A modulized approach gives you a structure to systematically build those powerful relationships. You'll develop a greater sense of purpose when you have a system you believe in and are proud of.

"Clients have peace of mind because their focus is on the plan rather than short-term volatility. You have an opportunity to WOW your client on a regular basis, and that, my boy, gives you the power to leverage your existing book."

"Awesome!" I said.

Henry suddenly whisked into the room. I noticed he wasn't carrying my packet, and he looked troubled. I'd never seen such grave concern on his face before. "Sir, I'm very sorry to interrupt."

"It's fine, Henry. We were just finishing up."

He hurried over to Victor and whispered something in his ear. Victor's face hardened. He immediately rose and said, "I apologize, Luke, but I'm afraid I must cut our meeting short. Please excuse me. Henry will show you out and give you your packet."

Before I could even respond, he was in the adjoining room. The door shut behind him.

CHAPTER TO-DO LIST

1. Build your business model around Financial Planning.

    *   A comprehensive financial plan takes the client's focus off of performance and short-term volatility and puts it on the plan.

    *   It gives the client peace of mind knowing there is a process at work rather than what may appear to be a random approach to their finances.

    *   It allows the advisor to see where all the assets are and to make decisions based on the client's complete financial picture rather than being forced to take a piecemeal approach to their finances.

2. Evaluate your discovery process.

    *   Don't shortchange the subjective questioning.

    *   Subjective questioning gives insight as to what's really important to the client and is valuable if and when adjustments must be made.

    *   Review Henry's list of subjective questions on the website.

3. Modulize.

    *   Decide which areas you feel are most important to a comprehensive planning process.

- Develop a list of your modules with a brief synopsis of each and submit to Compliance for approval.

- Laminate your module list and give it to the client.

- Present one to two modules per year depending on the client's timing and circumstances.

- Develop a spreadsheet to keep track of where clients are in your process.

- Keep a separate spreadsheet for each client and enter the date and notes each time you complete a module for the client.

For Additional Resources, go to:

www.executivetransformations.com/ plateau2pinnacle-additionalresources

8. THE INVESTMENT MANAGEMENT PROCESS

*"When you catch a glimpse of your potential,
that's when passion is born."*

— Zig Ziglar

Joe and I had plans to meet this week, but I'd been so busy, I was afraid I wouldn't be able to squeeze it in. When Henry called in the morning asking if I could push my meeting with Victor back a couple of hours, I was relieved. I'd had to postpone my lunch with him a couple of weeks ago and vowed not do it again. I immediately called him and confirmed our lunch appointment.

He usually had a ton of questions for me about my time with Victor and stayed on the edge of his seat, anxious to hear every detail. I noticed though, whenever I tried to ask him questions about Victor, he either didn't answer or was very vague.

My curiosity finally got the best of me, and today, I was determined to push him harder for answers. We met at his favorite restaurant, a hole-in-the-wall spot close to the river.

The place was filled with longshoremen. Several were clients, but I drew suspicious stares from the rest, until they saw I was with Joe. Then I was just one of the guys. Everybody knew Joe, and there was an endless procession of guys stopping by our table to say hello.

A lot of them made well over $100,000 a year, had nice pensions coming to them from the union, and had managed to accumulate quite a bit in their 401Ks. They were great clients because they always followed your advice, and once you were in, you could get referrals. That's how Ben and I had built our business in the beginning, thanks to Joe. And thanks to Victor and his demographic segmentation process, it was officially my new natural niche.

We had our typical lunch—huge portions of heavy comfort food. It was probably a good thing for both of us we only made it there twice a month. I don't think there was a salad on the menu, and even if there was, I wouldn't have dared order it.

Joe had an insatiable sweet tooth, and by the time his second slice of pecan pie heaped with vanilla ice cream arrived, I was ready with my questions. And today, I was going to get my answers.

I knew he probably wouldn't remember much about our conversation from the night of Ben's celebration party, so I began with an innocent open-ended question. "So, Joe, how did you and Victor meet?"

"Fate," he said without looking up from his pie.

My jaw dropped. "What did you say?" When I'd asked Henry the same question, he'd given me the exact same answer!

"Fate," he repeated, except this time he paused to look up from his pie.

"What does that mean? Fate?" I asked, frustrated.

He shrugged and licked his fingers. Satisfied, he leaned back in his chair and motioned for the check.

"I'm paying." I said bluntly, then pleaded, "C'mon, Joe. I'm making these huge changes in my business model based on the advice of somebody I barely know. What's the big secret about Victor Guise? Is he an arms dealer? In the Mafia? What?"

"Don't be ridiculous," he answered. Then he lowered his voice like he was about to divulge a national security secret. "You wanna know? I'll tell you, okay? The day I met Victor my life changed and for the good. It was one of those moments... what do you call it?"

"A defining moment?" I offered.

"Yeah, a defining moment. That's what it was all right. I was maybe 20, if that. Betty and I had just gotten married, and Ben was on the way. I'd lost my job that day. Only job I ever lost in my life...Asshole! Anyway, I'm sitting in this dive — not another soul in the joint. I made sure I was someplace I wouldn't run into anybody I knew. I don't even know the name of the place or where it was. A defining moment and you don't even remember where you were. Weird, huh?"

I nodded. Now I was the one on the edge of my seat.

Joe continued. "Anyway, I'm sitting there, wondering what the hell I'm going to do — how we're going to make it. I got no money, no job, and a baby on the way. So I'm sitting at the bar by myself, literally crying in my beer. I look up and there's Victor, sitting right next to me. Never saw him walk in, never heard him sit down, nothing. He just appeared."

"Then what happened?" I asked, hanging on his every word. My mind flashed back to the day Victor had disappeared, just like Joe was describing. I hadn't heard him or saw him leave. I'd just looked up and he was gone.

"Well, we get to talking, and I start telling him my story, and I just break down. He's quiet — doesn't say a word. He pulls out this fancy handkerchief. First time I ever saw anything made of silk, and I remember it had this sideways 8 on it."

"You mean the infinity symbol?" I asked, remembering the monogram on the handkerchief Victor handed me in the limo. I thought it was an 8 at first too, but now I realized it must have been a ∞, the infinity symbol.

"I don't know. I guess," Joe said, a little choked up. "Anyway, he hands it to me. I start crying like a baby. Of course, I feel like some kind of pansy, and I'm all apologizing and stuff. I start blubbering about my potential and how I never get a break."

Joe paused and cleared his throat. "Then he asks me if I want to change. I'm thinking what a stupid question. Hell yeah, I wanna change! Then he starts telling me there's a price. I get all PO'd and tell him I got no money, no job, and that's why we're having this stupid conversation anyway."

I knew exactly what Joe was going to say next. It had taken me this long to get answers. I wasn't about to interrupt.

"Then he says the price doesn't have anything to do with money. So then I think, 'What's this guy want?' I think he's yanking my chain, like he's messing with me. I'm about ready to deck him. That's the kind of mood I'm in anyway. He can tell I'm pissed, but he couldn't care less. He tells me that most people aren't willing to put in the time and effort to be successful. So I tell him, 'Well, I ain't most people!'"

"Then what did he say?" I asked in the most casual tone I could muster.

Joe gulped down what was left of the lukewarm coffee still on the table. "So then he looks me straight in the eye and says, and I'll never forget it: 'Real success is not just measured in dollars. It's measured in the lives you touch, the difference you make, and what you give back.' I've tried to live my life by those words ever since."

"Then what?" I could hardly contain myself.

"Then he asks me if I still wanna change, and I say, 'Hell yeah!' So he gives me a fifty-dollar bill and tells me to take my wife out to dinner and tell her I got a new job. I couldn't believe it! Fifty dollars was a lot of money back then. Shit, our rent wasn't much more than that. Anyway, then he says to meet him at 5:00 a.m. in front of Grayson Barge. They were the biggest and the best. They had barges, inhaul vessels, tugs. They had it all, and they treated their guys real good. In those days, everybody wanted to work for them."

"What did you do?" I asked, trying to envision how Joe would react to such an unusual encounter.

"I ask him, 'What about the hiring hall?' Everybody had to go through the union's hiring hall for work. Back then I was what they call a casual worker, which meant I was last in line. The good jobs all went to the union guys first. But Victor says, 'Don't worry about it, just be in front of Grayson at 5:00 a.m.' Well, that was unheard of, but I had nothing else going for me."

"So you met him at 5:00 a.m.?"

"Damn straight I did. I wasn't going to take the money — even though I needed it. But then he said I needed to do *exactly* what he said to do. I remember I didn't like the way that sounded, but I didn't really have a choice."

"So what happened at Grayson?" I asked, mesmerized by Joe's story.

"Well, before we walk in, he tells me this is my college. He says I have to be a diligent student — learn it all and do it all. That's what he tells me. Then he walks right into Mr. Grayson's office — the old man himself. He introduces me. Mr. Grayson shakes my hand and thanks Victor over and over — like I'm some great catch or something. So for the next seven years, I work for Grayson and I do just what Victor said. If anything needs to be done, I do it. If they need anything, I volunteer. As soon as I learn one thing, the old man puts me on something else. And that's where I really learned the business."

"Wow, that's some story, Joe," I said, wondering how Victor knew so much about so many things and had so many connections. How does a guy do that? He couldn't have been that much older than Joe in those days. And to command that kind of respect on the docks had to be unusual.

"But you said when you got your own business, he helped you systematize it, and that's when it took off. Did you keep in touch with him?" I asked.

"Never saw him or talked to him again until seven years later — to the day. At the end of my shift, Mr. Grayson calls me into his office, and there's Victor. The old man doesn't say anything, but Victor tells me that my time at Grayson is up."

"You must have freaked," I said. Joe had mellowed quite a bit, but when Ben and I were kids, he could have a real temper.

"You better believe it. I'm furious and yelling at Victor the whole way out. He ignores me until we get outside, and then just as calm as ever, he turns to me and says, 'You must do exactly as I say.'"

"Geez, Joe. What happened then?" I asked, surprised Joe didn't kill him on the spot.

"He tells me that I know the business now, and it's time to start my own. Well, I think the guy's lost his mind. I have two kids now and another one on the way. I'd managed to put some money away, but nothing close to what I needed to start a business. Besides, I knew *the* business but not anything about how to run *a* business."

Now I understood Joe's loyalty to Victor. Joe had definitely done the work, but Victor had made it all happen for him. I couldn't believe what I was hearing.

"He had me take out all my savings except for a small emergency fund and made me sign a promissory note to him for the rest. We found this old building that was falling apart, but it was in a great location, right there on the river. I fixed it up and set up shop. Victor arranged for me to buy my first barge, and I was in business."

"So did he help you with the business side?"

"A little in the beginning, but I mostly picked it up as I went along. He never said anything, but I know he sent me my first couple of customers. I didn't see him for a long time after that. Somehow I managed to pay the bills every month, including my note to Victor. I just scraped by the first few years, but gradually it started to build. Then after several years of working 12–14 hours a day, I had so much business, I could barely handle it."

"And that's when he came in and helped you systematize?" I added.

"Yep. And the rest is history!"

"So how did he end up being your financial advisor?" I asked, curious as to how Victor found time to be a financial advisor with everything else he had going on.

"He had me start socking money away from the beginning, even when I couldn't afford it. Remember, I'd promised to do exactly as he said. Later on I found out he handled all the big money around town, not just on the docks. Why he took an interest in me, I'll never know," Joe admitted.

"I could say the same thing," I replied. "So you guys just stayed in touch all these years?"

"Not really. Once I was well-established, systematized, and really making money, he introduced me to a new financial advisor and said he was 'pursuing other interests' — I think that's how he put it. I didn't hear from him for a long time after that, but it's like he has a sixth sense or something. He got in touch with me right after you and Ben decided you were going to form your partnership."

"Did Ben know him?" I asked abruptly.

"Ben met him once when he was about 13 or 14. He really seemed to take a liking to Ben 'cause after that, Ben got birthday cards from him every year. I don't know what was in those birthday cards, but that's when Ben got real interested in stocks and finance and all that."

"I know he was married, but did he have kids?" I couldn't

stop myself. I was finally getting answers to my questions. "And what about Henry?"

"Never said a word about his private life to me, so I never asked. He's always been a real private guy, and everybody just respects that. It's kind of understood, if you know what I mean. He likes it that way. Supposedly his wife got cancer or something. I don't know exactly what happened, but she got real sick. Word on the street was he quit everything to take care of her, but she died after a couple of years. I don't know if he had kids or not. Like I said, he never talked about his private life.

"As for Henry, I know he helped Victor when his wife was sick. Come to think of it, I think he's been around for as long as I've known Victor. If you need to get in touch with Victor, you always go through Henry. That's the way it's always been."

I looked at my watch and had to do a double-take. "Oh, man, I'm going to be late." I snatched the bill from the table. Luckily I had cash on me, so I threw down enough to cover it.

"I have to go, Joe. I have to get up to Victor's. Thanks for sharing your story with me. I really appreciate it. I'll see you soon." I gave Joe a slap on the back and rushed out the door.

I screeched to a stop outside the huge house with one minute to spare, thankful I wasn't late. As I jogged up the gravel path to the house, I noticed Henry on the porch busily tending to the plants. By the time I reached the top of the stairs, I was more out of breath than I cared to admit. I chalked it up to the heavy meal rather than my only making it to the gym twice this week.

"Well, good afternoon, sir," called Henry. "In a hurry today, are we?" He smiled as he wiped his hands and then opened the door.

"Can't be late, Henry. That would be bad for my reputation," I joked.

"Well, we certainly wouldn't want you to tarnish your perfect punctuality record now, would we, sir?"

"Absolutely not," I answered as we walked toward the den. After hearing Joe's story, I felt somehow closer to Victor and Henry both—like I knew them better.

He opened the door to the den with his usual flair. Victor was in his favorite chair reading the *Financial Times*.

"Well, hello, my boy," he called as he stood and motioned me over. "Come, come have a seat."

"Thank you, sir," I said as I took my usual spot next to him.

"Now tell me, how was your week?" he asked.

"It was good. I got a lot done on the financial planning system, and I have to admit, the more I develop it, the more value I see it adds. In fact, I'm actually excited about beginning to use it as part of my business model."

"That's music to my ears," Victor said, delighted.

"I added some key subjective questions to my discovery process, and I spent a lot of time developing my actual modules. I have my spreadsheet all done and my list of B clients ready to go. I even have three appointments set up for next week. And when I called to tell them it was time we did a formal plan, they totally embraced the idea!"

"Excellent! Great work and tremendous progress!" He was beaming.

Just like last week, I could tell he was really proud of me, but I questioned whether he'd ever come right out and say it. My mind drifted back to Joe's story. Maybe he was always just business, and that was too personal of a comment for him. He seemed to have a more personal relationship with Ben though, even if it was just through the mail.

It was strange Ben never once mentioned him to me. I wondered what was in those birthday cards, if anything. I'd love to get my hands on them and read every one. Ben would have kept them all. That much I knew.

I was developing an obsession with learning more about Victor, the man. What drove him? How did he come to be so accomplished in so many different areas? I knew I could learn much more than business from Victor.

He'd lived and lived large. I'm sure over the years Joe's wasn't the only person whose life he'd changed in a big way. What did he see in the people whose lives he chose to touch? Did he see something in me, or was I just a favor to Joe…or Ben? These meetings were probably meant for Ben all along, and I was just part of the package. Suddenly I felt a familiar melancholy. I sighed heavily.

"Is something wrong, Luke?" Victor asked, concern in his voice.

"Uh, no, sir. I'm sorry. I was just thinking how much Ben would have enjoyed our meetings. After all, he was the one who was supposed to be here," I answered, staring blindly out the window.

Victor cocked his head and studied me for a long time before he replied. I could feel his ice-blue eyes boring right through me.

Finally, he said, "It was my original intention, Luke, that both of you would be present for our meetings. However, life often deals us an unexpected hand…in this case, Ben's premature death. Each of you possessed superior yet complementary gifts which I've been aware of for many years. Ben's gifts were neither greater nor lesser than your own.

"Potential…is virtually infinite. It grows as you grow. It's cultivated and nurtured by belief and action. Both must be present, which is why it remains the greatest untapped human resource there is in this world. When I choose to invest my energy in a certain individual, it's because I see a spark within them that has the ability to ignite their own infinite potential. My purpose is to ensure that yours does not go untapped. Do you understand?"

I turned from the window, knowing I'd just experienced my own defining moment. I looked him straight in the eye and, for the first time, equaled his intensity, a slow smile spreading across my face. "Yes, sir, I do."

"Good. Are you ready to get started then?"

"Absolutely. And thank you, sir," I added.

He smiled. "The privilege is all mine."

I took a deep breath and pulled my notebook and Victor pen from my briefcase. I felt energized and empowered like never before.

"Today we're going to talk about systematizing your investment management process. So tell me, what percentage of your business is currently fee-based?" he asked.

"Not as much as I'd like. I'd say about 35%. Now more is residualized because I have a lot of C share mutual funds and UITs. A lot of people just don't like seeing those quarterly fees."

"I see. And what platforms do you tend to use in fee-based accounts?"

"I use some Separately Managed Accounts, but mostly I use a platform we have that allows you to put most investments in, I run the money, and it's wrapped. I also have a lot of those mutual fund wrap accounts that get automatically rebalanced."

"And how many households do you have?" Victor asked, tapping his fingertips together.

"Right at 200," I replied. I knew he was setting me up to make a case for transitioning to more fee-based business. I knew it made sense, but I'd never really committed to it.

"Let's go back to 2008," he began. "And let's say you had a crystal ball and knew exactly what was about to happen in the market. What could you do about it?"

"Well, of course, I'd move most people to cash and change the allocation for others," I answered.

"And from a logistical standpoint, how exactly would you accomplish that? You have 200 households with, what would you say? About 1000 individual accounts?"

I nodded and sank down in my chair. Somehow I knew this was a debate I wasn't going to win.

"You probably have roughly 500 different mutual funds, ETFs and CEFs, of which approximately 150 are in only one account. Sixty-five percent of your assets are in brokerage accounts, and your managed assets are split among mutual fund wrap accounts, SMAs, and nondiscretionary advisory accounts. Where would you start?"

"I guess with my A clients," I mumbled.

"But in order to make *all* the changes you mentioned, basically you'd need to speak with roughly 500 individuals across your 200 households. As you're calling, how would you be sure to follow up with people you missed with the first call?" he pressed.

"It was chaos in 2008, I'll admit that. And you're right, I didn't really know where to start or how to get to everyone or even how to get a handle on what everybody had."

"The number of different positions you hold is not unusual. And how many Large Cap Value funds do you really need? This type of investment management also represents a significant liability to you if something blows up in a fund that you no longer follow."

"I know you're right, and that kind of liability really scares me. In fact in 2008, I had a lot of sleepless nights worrying about that," I admitted.

"Do you really want to face an arbitration panel and admit you weren't up to date or actively following the fund your client was invested in? Not to mention, have you ever thought about how many positions you have that you aren't getting paid a dime to manage?"

"Okay, okay, you made your point. I get it. You're right."

"As I mentioned last week, Luke, times have changed.

People want and need a plan because most recognize that the days of buying big companies and holding them forever are gone. The markets change quickly. You must have the ability to be tactical and change with them. Your clients hire you to manage their investments. The best and most efficient way of doing that is in a discretionary fee-based platform."

"Oh, I'm not sure if my clients would go for a discretionary platform," I said warily. "Isn't that taking on even more liability when it comes right down to it?"

"Not at all. Remember, there are really two types of discretion — firm discretion and advisor discretion. I would bet that most of your clients assume you already have discretion and are able to make changes as you see fit."

"Now that's probably true."

"In the event of market dislocations, it's physically impossible for you to make outgoing calls to all your clients. If you have 200 households, who wants to be the 200th household you call? Who are *you* going to choose to be the 200th?"

"Okay, I know you're right. I'm just not sure how many of my clients would feel comfortable giving someone else discretion over their accounts."

"Don't you think *they* deserve to make that decision?"

"I guess I shouldn't just assume they won't go for it," I admitted.

"Precisely. Managing client accounts under a discretionary platform based on risk profile and a defined investment matrix allows you to respond quickly and effectively to market changes. It's best for the client and it's best for you."

"It is best for them, and I'd actually get paid on a lot of assets I'm responsible for but have *never* gotten paid on."

"Furthermore, I see it as your *obligation* to have the conversation with your clients and make them understand the full ramifications of not moving to your discretionary model."

"I see the value. I really do, but this would be such a major shift in my business model, I wouldn't even know where to start," I said.

"Well, it just so happens I have some suggestions for you." Victor smiled. "Let's approach this systematically, shall we?"

"Geez, and I thought the financial planning was a lot of work! I had no idea you were going to spring this on me the very next week," I teased.

"Just look at it as moving toward that infinite potential of yours. If it were easy—"

"I know. Everybody would be doing it."

"Exactly. So I would suggest you begin by building your Investment Matrix. Pick two primary holdings in each of the primary style boxes. Large Cap, Mid Cap, and Small Cap, with growth, value, and balanced options in each. You should also have two backup managers you can use in special client situations—for instance, if a client doesn't like a particular fund company or if a long-term, favorite manager moves on."

I scribbled as fast as I could. "It would be a lot easier knowing a handful of stories per style instead of 400!"

"Now you're seeing the light! It also gives you an opportunity to build loyalty with your selected wholesalers. That way when you want to host an event, you have someone who'll be willing to help defray the costs."

"You have to like that idea."

"If your platform allows it, have one or two low-cost ETFs for each style, as a cost-reducing alternative. In addition to the primary style boxes, pick one or two investments in the secondary style boxes. These should include things like REITs, managed futures, and alternatives."

I meticulously wrote down everything Victor suggested. I knew I would need every suggestion he gave me if I was going to do this right.

"Also, pick one or two investments in the satellite styles. These should include sector funds, international, and anything else you feel is appropriate."

Victor paused and let me catch up to him with my notes. I took the opportunity to stretch my hand, which was starting to cramp.

"Ready," I said. "Is that pretty much it for the Investment Matrix?"

"Yes. That process is actually going to be easier than it may first appear because many of your selections you'll already be familiar with."

"True. I'm not overwhelmed yet." I smiled.

"Excellent. The next thing you'll need to do is build your platform model. This is where you'll decide what platforms you're going to use for small accounts, midsized accounts, and large accounts. First you'll have to decide how you'll define each tier of account from an asset perspective."

"You mean like small accounts are below $250,000, mid are $250,000 to $1,000,000, and large are over $1,000,000?"

"Yes. And this will be different for every advisor. In fact, your entire investment management process should be unique to you, using your current book as a guideline. Also, remember that these breakpoints will change as your business grows. Today, your large accounts may be those over $1,000,000 in assets, but a couple of years from now that breakpoint may rise to over $3,000,000."

"So the basic infrastructure will remain the same but almost everything else will probably change over time?"

"Exactly. Now once you've decided on your asset breakpoints, you must next decide what platforms you will use for each. For instance, you may decide to use a firm discretionary model with a mutual fund wrap for small accounts. And for large accounts, you may decide on SMAs or your own advisor discretionary portfolio management account implementing your own model portfolios based on risk tolerance."

"Okay, so the second step is building my platform model. What's next?"

"Next you're going to build your risk-based model portfolios. This is actually a two-part process as well. First you'll create an asset allocation model for each risk profile. Begin with your core allocation models—conservative, moderate, and aggressive. Then you may want to add a taxable income and tax-free model. Later on, you might want to add an ultraconservative or moderately aggressive. What allocation models you choose to build is up to you, but they should be based on what you deem is most appropriate for your book."

"I think I'm going to keep it as simple as possible, at least in the beginning."

"Good idea. In the second part of the process, you'll build your actual risk-based model portfolios by using the managers in your Investment Matrix to implement your asset allocation models."

"I'm writing as fast as I can, and I think I've got it all so far, but please tell me Henry has the entire process outlined in my packet today!"

Victor laughed. "Indeed he does. Have I overwhelmed you yet?"

"Not yet, but we're definitely approaching the saturation point."

"Bear with me just a bit longer. So you've built your Investment Matrix, your Platform Model, and your Risk-Based Model Portfolios. Next you'll build your pricing matrix, and again, this is completely up to you. And let me just say that there are probably as many pricing models as there are financial advisors."

"I know the key number is 1%. That's what you want to average, but can you give me a couple of examples of what advisors base their pricing on?"

"I'd be glad to, but first let me say this. The most important thing to remember is you want to develop a pricing matrix that is fair to the client and is a true reflection of the value you bring to the client. You must believe that you are worth every penny you charge and *be* worth every penny you charge. If you have conviction on your pricing, so will clients. If you don't, neither will they. Once you decide on your pricing matrix, put it in writing and adhere to it. Understood?"

"Yes, sir," I replied.

"Good. Now, obviously pricing is going to be based on assets with some sort of sliding scale and utilizing breakpoints. I have heard of advisors who use different pricing structures for equities only, fixed income only, and balanced accounts. I've heard other advisors use a single sliding scale for all asset classes. I've also heard of advisors using a blended scale. For example, they charge a certain percentage for the first $500,000, another for the next $500,000, and another for the next $1,000,000, eventually reaching a negotiated rate. Some advisors wrap fixed income, and others utilizing ladders hold fixed income outside the wrapped account. It is all dependent on what resonates with you and what you feel comfortable with."

"Wow, you weren't kidding. There are a lot different pricing models out there! This is going to take some serious thought and number crunching on my part."

"I'm sure you're up to the task. Now let's talk about implementation."

"So that's it. We're done building the actual system?"

"We are. As far as implementation goes, you must be committed to your new business model without exception. All new clients go into your new discretionary business model or they don't become clients. Anything short of that is not true commitment. Do you understand?"

"Yes, sir. But—"

"No buts, Luke. It's nonnegotiable. Remember, *exactly* as I say," Victor said sternly.

"Yes, sir."

"Now, let's address implementation relative to existing clients. It is in your client's best interest to make this change with you. If you have the proper conviction when presenting it to existing clients, most will clearly see the value and make the change."

"I think I'm going to present it just the way you presented it to me using the 2008 example. Like you said, no one is going to want to be number 200, and I don't want them to be number 200!"

"I think that's a splendid idea," said Victor.

"What about if I have some clients that just won't do it?"

"That probably needs to be considered on a case-by-case basis. However, I can assure you that eventually — perhaps not in the beginning, but eventually — you will find that you no longer wish to work with clients who do not appreciate the value your business model offers."

I nodded. "Yep, I can see that happening — eventually."

"When converting existing clients, I would begin with IRAs that pose no taxable consequences. Then I would move to taxable accounts that will bear little to no tax consequences as a result of the change. The taxable accounts that will suffer significant tax consequences will take more time and effort. I would suggest that you move them to your discretionary platform immediately. However, move them toward your actual models gradually as you are able through tax selling and other strategies that make sense for the client."

"So move them to the platform but only to the model as it makes sense for them?" I clarified.

"Correct. And that, my boy, is how you systematize your investment management process," said Victor. "I realize we covered a lot of rather technical material today. Do you have any questions?"

"No, sir. I think it makes sense — as long as Henry has this all outlined in my packet!"

"Indeed, I do," called Henry from the door, packet in hand.

"There he is," said Victor as he stood and stretched.

I did the same and then shook Victor's hand. "Thank you, sir," I said earnestly. I looked him straight in the eye for the second time today. "Thank you — for *everything.*"

"You are quite welcome, my boy — for *everything.*"

CHAPTER TO-DO LIST

1. Reread the Case for Discretionary Platforms.

2. Build your Investment Matrix.

    *   Pick two primary holdings in the primary style boxes — Large Cap, Mid Cap, Small Cap — Value, Growth, and Balanced in each.

    *   Pick two backup holdings in each primary style box.

    *   Pick primary investments in the secondary style boxes — REITs, managed futures, alternatives.

    *   Pick primary investments in satellite styles — sector funds, international.

3. Build your Platform Model.

    *   Establish your breakpoints for small, mid, and large accounts.

    *   Decide what platforms you will use for each tier of account.

4. Build your Risk-based Model Portfolios.

    *   Create your asset allocation models for each risk profile.

    *   Build your model portfolios by using the managers within your Investment Matrix to implement your asset allocation models.

5. Build your Pricing Matrix.

    - It should be fair to the client and an accurate reflection of the value you bring to the client.

    - Develop conviction that you are worth every penny and be worth every penny.

6. Implementation

    - Use your discretionary business model with all new clients without exception.

    - Existing clients

        ➢ Begin with IRAs — no tax consequences

        ➢ Taxable accounts with little or no tax consequences

        ➢ Taxable accounts with significant tax consequences

            ▪ Move to your discretionary platform immediately.

            ▪ Move toward your models as you can as it makes sense to the client through tax selling and other appropriate strategies.

For Additional Resources, go to:

**www.executivetransformations.com/
plateau2pinnacle-additionalresources**

9. REVOLUTIONARY PROSPECTING

"Innovation is taking two things and putting them together in a new way."

— Tom Freston

My financial planning appointments had gone very well. I was working on three plans, all at different stages of the process. Sending Henry's letter listing exactly what the client needed to bring with them had been a stroke of genius. I'd even taken it one step further and had my assistant make sure they had everything together when she called to confirm the appointment. That allowed me to gather all the information I needed to run the plan in the first meeting.

I'd done a practice plan on Aimee and me, and it had taken a long time. I was hoping these would go quicker as I got used to the system. Once I caught up, my goal was to set at least one financial planning appointment a week.

Setting up my new discretionary model had been extremely time-consuming. In fact, there was no way I'd be done by the time I headed over to Victor's today. It was important I did it right, so I wasn't rushing through it.

I was so focused on putting together my model portfolios, I didn't even hear Randy come in and sit down. He cleared his throat to get my attention. Surprised, I looked up from the pile of papers I had spread all over my desk.

"Well, I hit it," he announced.

"Hit what?" I asked. I had absolutely no clue what he was talking about.

"Just $10,000 gross, that's all." He was smiling from ear to ear.

I put down my pen, walked around my desk, and shook his hand. "Congratulations, Randy! That's awesome!" He was so thrilled, his excitement was contagious. "You're a real advisor now!"

"Thanks, Luke. When you told me a few months ago that once you hit the $10,000 mark you never looked back, I was determined to get there—even though I had no idea how."

"How did you?" I asked.

"I just did what you said. One of my buddies was the property manager at that new retirement community. You know the one by the old nine-hole golf course?"

I nodded.

"It's really nice, by the way. Anyway, my friend set me up to do weekly investment seminars up there. It didn't cost me anything, so I did an eight-week series. At first only a couple of people showed up. But I remembered what you said about not doubting myself and how anything would work as long as I worked it consistently. So that's what I did. About six weeks into it, some of the old guys started asking me to play golf with them, and I took some of the ladies out to lunch, and it just started to build."

"I'm proud of you, Randy. Not many guys make it, you know."

"Yeah, I know. There's only me, two girls, and one other guy left from our training class."

"So do you feel different?" I asked, smiling.

"I kind of do," he replied. "Definitely not as paranoid."

I glanced at the clock on the wall. "Listen, I can't today because I have a meeting, but I want to take you to lunch to celebrate tomorrow, okay?"

"Thanks, Luke. That would be good."

"Great. Pencil me in," I said as I grabbed my briefcase and hurried to catch the elevator.

"You got it," he called after me.

I rang the doorbell and was taken aback when Victor answered the door. "Hello, Luke! Come in, come in. Did you have a good week?"

"Uh, yes, sir, but where's Henry? I wasn't expecting *you* to answer the door."

"Henry stepped out. He'll be back shortly," said Victor. "And contrary to what you may believe, I am fully capable of answering my own door."

"Oh no, sir, I didn't mean it like that," I answered, flustered.

He laughed. "Oh, my boy. You're far too serious for this beautiful day."

Victor seemed in an unusually good mood today. Not that he was ever in a bad mood. He just seemed different—more casual. *Maybe a man just has to open his own door sometimes,* I thought.

"It's unseasonably warm outside and, as we've established, a beautiful day. What would you say to a change of venue and we have our discussion on the back porch?" he asked.

"Sure," I said. "That sounds great."

I followed him down the wide hall to the very back of the house. Victor flung open the glass doors. I think he was trying to imitate Henry's flair, but it just didn't work for him.

We walked onto a spacious screened porch with high ceilings and what looked to be very comfortable chairs.

Henry must have left recently because there was an ice-cold pitcher of his strawberry lemonade and glasses sitting on a table between two of the chairs. "Have a seat," said Victor as he poured us each a glass of what had become one of my all-time favorite beverages.

The porch overlooked a massive pool with weathered stone dragons on each end spitting a slow but steady stream of water into it. The pool must have had a dark bottom because it looked more like a lake than a typical in-ground swimming pool. Behind it, I noticed the helipad where I assumed Victor caught his "rides." Beyond that, there were rolling green hills as far as the eye could see.

"So tell me about your week," said Victor.

"It was good. I have to admit, I love my new financial planning process, and I think clients love it even more than I do. This week, I did a plan for Rebecca. Remember she was the lady who divorced that jerk of a C client I wanted to fire when I first started my client contact schedule."

"As I recall, she brought you a $500,000 check as a result of that call."

"That's Rebecca." I grinned. "Well, guess what I uncovered?"

"Judging from the smile on your face, I'd say additional assets, perhaps?"

"$826,000 to be exact. It's in her 401K, *and* she's retiring in April! Is that awesome or what?"

"Indeed."

"I really do think the process gives clients more peace of mind, and it shows you where all the assets are! I'm working on three plans right now, and I've found additional assets with every single one."

"And—let's not forget. In the case of Rebecca, it all began with your client contact schedule. Excellent work, my boy!"

Victor nodded with satisfaction. "Now — how's the investment management process faring?"

"I spent a lot of time working on it this week. I'm just about done with my model portfolios."

"It's a thought-intensive, time-consuming process," he acknowledged. "And not one that can be rushed. However, it sounds like you're making good progress."

"I think I'll be done with it by next week — at least my first attempt. I'm sure it'll need to be tweaked a little."

"Well, you'll be pleased to know that the upcoming week will be somewhat of a break for you." Victor smiled.

"How so?"

"This week we're going to discuss the acquisition of new business."

"You mean prospecting? Every advisor's favorite topic," I grunted.

"Ah, do I detect a note of sarcasm there? The good news is I won't be asking you to cold-call or other such nonsense."

"Whew! That is good news," I said relieved.

"I've already given you the tools you need to effectively leverage your existing book for additional assets and referrals on a regular basis. I expect most of your new business to come as a result of consistent implementation of those systems — referrals, client contact, branding, and financial planning. After all, warm is always better than cold. Would you agree?"

"Absolutely," I answered.

He continued, "Therefore, I'm not going to spend time on cold prospecting. What I am going to do is give you another possible source of introductions should you choose to pursue it."

"Okay, so this is like optional?" I asked.

"In a manner of speaking. I would recommend you spend a modest amount of time each week on this methodology to supplement your primary sources of new business."

I opened my briefcase and pulled out what Aimee called

my "Victor tools of Victory" — my pen and notebook. Aimee definitely had a corny streak, but I loved her in spite of it. She liked to remind me that corny sells, and most of the time she was right.

"I'm ready," I said as enthusiastically as possible.

"All right. Today we're going to discuss LinkedIn. Specifically, we'll be talking about how to use a relatively new technology to acquire old-fashioned introductions. Do you have a LinkedIn profile?"

I was surprised Victor knew anything at all about LinkedIn, but then I guess I shouldn't have been. He was, after all, Victor.

"Yes, I do. When the firm first let us start using LinkedIn, they gave us very stringent rules on what we could and couldn't put in our profile. So I did one and got it approved. I have probably about 30 or so connections."

"If you haven't updated your profile recently, it likely does not include your conditioning phrase. You must add that and be sure it's in a prominent place. If possible, include it in your profile more than once."

"Got it." I scribbled a note to myself so I wouldn't forget.

"And you have a link from your profile to your website, correct?" he asked.

"I'm sure I do, but I'll double-check when I get back to the office."

"And a professional photo?"

"Yes, sir."

"Good. You'd be surprised how many people have photos with their dog or child. Even though it's a social media site, it is for professionals, so it's important that you conduct yourself as such at all times."

"Yes, sir. If you don't mind me asking, are you on LinkedIn?"

"Of course I am. You have to stay up with the times, my boy."

"Then I'll have to send you a connection notice."

"Please do," he said. "I'm sure you're aware that there are all kinds of tools at your disposal on the site—groups you can join, company pages you can follow, and upgrades you can buy. If you were a new advisor, I'd suggest you become an expert on LinkedIn and utilize it almost exclusively to build your business. For new advisors, it's a revolutionary prospecting tool!"

I made a note to ask Randy if he used it for prospecting. He was young and tech savvy, so I was sure he did, but maybe I'd get some ideas from Victor I could share with him.

"So how will a seasoned geezer like me use it?" I laughed.

"It needs to remain relatively simple for 'geezers' such as ourselves." He winked and then continued, "As I mentioned earlier, the first step is to commit a modest amount of time each week to developing your LinkedIn system."

"What's a modest amount of time?"

"That depends on how much you plan to use the system I lay out for you. If you plan on utilizing the system on a weekly basis, I'd suggest 45–60 minutes per week. That's virtually nothing in 'Internet time.'"

"You're right about that," I agreed.

"In the beginning, you'll use that time to build your connections. Once you have a substantial number of connections, then you'll use your time to review their connections or your second-degree connections. You'll be looking for people you feel have the potential to be good clients."

"So you mean like attorneys or CPAs or people in management?"

"Exactly. Also, people who have worked for the same company for many years or someone who just left a company after many years would both be good potential candidates."

"Small business owners too," I added.

"Now you're thinking, my boy!"

"Okay, so I go through my connections' connections and make a list of potential prospects. Then what do I do?"

"Remember, I said we were going to use this technology to acquire old-fashioned introductions. I suggest you schedule one LinkedIn lunch per week with a connection of yours. At that lunch, you will explain that you are just getting involved with LinkedIn and you noticed that they have x number of connections. Spend some time talking to them about that. Put them in an advisory role. People love to give advice. I suppose I'm living proof of that." He laughed.

"So I should ask maybe how long they've been on LinkedIn and did they make a concerted effort to build those connections or did they just kind of happen—stuff like that?"

"Correct. Whatever you're curious about, ask. Then let them know that a few of their connections caught your attention. Plan on arriving at the meeting with four to six on your list and review everyone on the list with them."

"I guess everyone on LinkedIn is on there for the same reason."

"Correct again. The beauty of LinkedIn is that it allows you to be much more direct with people when it comes to referrals and introductions, rather than having to do the delicate referral dance you typically do as a financial advisor."

"I never thought of it like that. This could be a gold mine for prospecting!"

Victor eyed me and then said, "It's not my intention to burst your bubble but rather realign your expectations with reality. LinkedIn is revolutionary and can be an effective method for acquiring new business. However, it is not a magic bullet."

"It seems like a slam dunk to me," I answered.

"Not so fast, my boy. As you go through the list with your connection, be prepared for responses, such as 'They know nothing about LinkedIn and have no idea how they got on there at all.'"

"That's ridiculous!" I snapped.

"True. However, you will hear that on occasion. Also, be prepared for some to inform you that they don't know the person you're inquiring about at all, which could be an entirely accurate statement."

I could feel my short-lived enthusiasm fading. "So what you're saying is it's really not any different than any other form of prospecting. You have to kiss a lot of frogs."

"That's one way of putting it, but, Luke, you should know by now that there is no magic bullet! However, using LinkedIn is a much more direct and efficient method of acquiring introductions. Many people when put in an advisory role will tell you the truth. They will tell you if someone on your list has no money or is not someone you care to work with or perhaps they are someone you should talk to. When you find one of those, ask for an introduction."

"So just come right out and ask for the introduction?" I asked.

"Absolutely. Again, put them in an advisory role. Tell them that this person is someone you'd like to meet. What do they think would be the best way of doing that? And don't make them do all the work and figure it all out themselves. Give them some suggestions. Perhaps you could take them both to lunch or give the person a call and use your connection's name or have them introduce you via LinkedIn."

"They can do that? Give an introduction on LinkedIn?"

"Indeed they can. Even the free LinkedIn account allows you to make several introductions at a time. As long as the person you wish to be introduced to is a second- or third-degree connection, the 'Get Introduced' link will appear on their profile."

"Really? I guess I need to spend a little time on the site and figure some things out. Doing one LinkedIn lunch a week is something I could set up without much effort, and if I end up with one good introduction every four to six weeks, it would be a win."

"As I said, I expect most of your new business to come from leveraging your existing book, but LinkedIn can serve as another arrow in your quiver, so to speak."

"I agree with you. If I was a rookie, I'd be using it a lot, but using the systems we've already set up is going to keep me busy for a long time. I'll commit to doing one LinkedIn lunch a week and see what happens. It can't hurt."

"Now there's one other topic I'd like to touch on, and that's having a structured drip system for prospects, regardless of their origin. Do you have one?"

"Well, I wouldn't say it was structured. I have all my prospects and referrals on a spreadsheet. If they're hot, I call them regularly. If they're not hot, I call when I get around to it, which to be honest isn't all that often."

"I think a bit more structure is in order," he said firmly. "What you have to remember with any prospect is the probability of connecting with them at precisely the time they're ready to do business is relatively low. Therefore, it becomes essential to keep your name in front of them so they don't forget about you. They may not be ready to do business today or next month or even six months from now. However, if you have maintained contact with them and have provided valuable information on an ongoing basis, when they are ready, you will be the one they remember."

"I know. That's Financial Advisor 101 stuff. It's just once you have a decent-sized book, you spend most of your time with your existing clients."

"I understand. That's why we want the foundation of the drip system to be on autopilot, so to speak."

"I'm sure you have some suggestions?"

"As a matter of fact, I do. Most firms have some sort of automated newsletter available. Typically, they have your picture, phone number, and a link to your website. They also include different articles each month. Does your firm have something similar?"

"Probably. I think so. It would be easy enough to find out."

"Keep in mind from a Compliance standpoint, the automated newsletter cannot be your first contact with a prospect. However, once they've agreed that you may keep in touch with them from time to time and you have their e-mail address, usually all you need to do is add them to the distribution list and it goes out automatically each month. And of course they can unsubscribe at any time."

"You think people really read those things?" I asked.

"That, my boy, is irrelevant. The point is, if they remain on the list and don't unsubscribe, they see your name on a monthly basis. That's our primary objective."

"That makes sense. It probably wouldn't be a bad idea to send that to clients as well."

"I think that would be a splendid idea. And if by chance your firm doesn't have anything like that available, there are many e-newsletter services that will do the very same thing. For a price, of course. Often, these outside firms offer more flexibility and customization in that you have a choice of articles you wish to include."

"That's the autopilot side of it, but I still need to call them periodically. I've heard all kinds of different recommendations on how often you should call. How often do you think I should call a prospect if they're not hot?"

"That's an excellent question. Ideally, you want to call them often enough that they remember who you are when you call but not so much as to annoy them. For a prospect with no perceived immediate potential, I would say every eight weeks. Quarterly is not often enough, monthly is too much. You may want to experiment in that sweet spot of six to eight weeks."

I scribbled down six to eight weeks in my notebook. "So I generally call them with different ideas or to invite them to an event. Is there any other reason to call them?"

"Unless you are familiar with their particular situation, how can you possibly call them with an idea?"

"Well, you know if there's something virtually everyone should have in their portfolio."

"And how often is that truly the case?"

"Not very often I guess," I muttered.

"You want to mix it up. Inviting them to events is good. Pure goodwill calls are excellent as well. This would be a call where you just call to check in with them and see if there's anything you can help with. One of the best questions you can ask a prospect is 'What are you most concerned with in your portfolio right now?'"

"The old hot button question."

"Exactly. The objective of a prospecting call is really twofold. First, you want to come away with a legitimate reason to call them again in the future, and second, you want each call to get progressively warmer by taking the time to build rapport whenever possible."

"Hmm. This kind of explains why I don't turn a lot of prospects into clients."

"Also, there's always a holiday around the corner. Capitalize on those to build rapport."

"I'm good at getting the business when I have hot prospects, but building rapport over time with a regular prospect—probably not so good."

"We all have areas in which we can improve." Victor smiled.

I sipped the last of my lemonade as we both stared out at the rolling hills now silhouetted by the fading sun. Henry gently opened the doors to the right of us.

"Excuse me, sir."

"Yes, Henry. Come in. We're just finishing up."

"I wanted to inform you that I've returned from the airport, and your guest is awaiting your presence in the den."

"Thank you, Henry. Please let her know that I'll be joining

her momentarily."

"Of course, sir."

Victor turned to face me as he stood. "I suggest my boy that you take full advantage of what's left of this beautiful day. Henry will have your packet for you at the front door."

"Yes sir, I will. Thank you," I said and wondered who was waiting in the den.

CHAPTER TO-DO LIST

1. Your LinkedIn profile

    -   Build or update your profile to include your con-
        ditioning phrase—display it prominently and
        preferably more than once.

    -   Be sure there is a link from your profile to your
        website.

    -   Always use a professional photograph.

2. Using LinkedIn to acquire old-fashioned introductions

    -   Allocate a specific amount of time to Linked-In
        each week—the amount of time you allocate is
        dependent on how active you will be in using the
        site for gaining introductions.

    -   Plan on a minimum of 45–60 minutes each week.

        ➢   Begin by adding a substantial number of con-
            nections.

        ➢   Once you've built your number of connections,
            each week, review your connections' connec-
            tions or your second-degree connections.

        ➢   Determine your criteria for identifying po-
            tential introductions.

            ▪   Professionals

            ▪   Individuals in upper and middle man-
                agement positions

- Individuals who have worked for the same company for many years

- Individuals who work for a company that employs several of your current clients

- Individuals who recently left a company after being employed for many years

- Small business owners

- Individuals who enjoy expensive hobbies — sailing, golf, etc.

➢ Set one LinkedIn lunch per week with one of your connections.

- Bring a list of four to six of their connections you'd like to review with them for potential introductions.

- Begin by discussing their LinkedIn experience and their connections in general terms.

- Review the list with them.

- Put your connection in an advisory role on how best to reach a potential introduction.

- When you receive positive feedback on a certain individual, ask for the introduction but offer them options on how best to reach that individual.

  o Lunch with both your connection and their connection

   o Phone call using your connection's name

   o Invitation for both to your next event

   o LinkedIn introduction

3. Keep expectations in line with reality.

- LinkedIn is a revolutionary prospecting tool but not a magic bullet.

- Be prepared for responses such as the following:

  ➤ They don't know how they ended up on LinkedIn.

  ➤ They don't know the connection you're referencing.

  ➤ They don't know the person you're referencing, but they'll give you the names of some people you should call.

  ➤ The person you're referencing doesn't have any money.

  ➤ The person you're referencing is not someone you'd want to work with.

  ➤ The person you're referencing is someone you should talk to.

4. Develop a structured drip process for all prospects regardless of their origin.

- The foundation of the drip should be on autopilot.

- ➤ Use firm-sponsored or outside e-newsletter service to have an e-newsletter sent automatically to all clients and prospects.

- ➤ An e-newsletter cannot be your first contact with someone.

- If the prospect is not hot or does not have any perceived immediate potential, call every six to eight weeks.

- Mix up your calls.

  - ➤ Goodwill/Check-in calls

  - ➤ Holiday calls to build rapport

  - ➤ Provide information on a particular concern of theirs.

  - ➤ Invite to an event or outing

- Primary objectives for prospecting calls

  - ➤ Come away with a legitimate reason for calling them again.

  - ➤ Make each consecutive call warmer by building rapport—goodwill, check-in, holiday calls.

For Additional Resources, go to:

**www.executivetransformations.com/
plateau2pinnacle-additionalresources**

10. TRACKING

"Vision without execution is just hallucination."
— Henry Ford

I was seriously craving Henry's strawberry lemonade as I turned onto the heavily camouflaged road leading back to Victor's home. It had taken many visits to the place before I no longer missed its secret entry. Now I breezed onto the road without even thinking. *Kind of like Batman heading to the Batcave,* I mused.

A lot had changed since those early visits in September. Here we were starting December, and my business had come a long way. *I* had come a long way. For the first time in my 10-year career, my practice looked, felt, and acted like a real business. I'd easily blown through the production number I had to hit this year, a number that seemed impossible just a few months ago. Under Victor's tutelage, I was already stretching for my next breakpoint and fully expected to get there before year-end.

I parked the car in my usual spot. The year was almost over, and darkness was sneaking in earlier and earlier each day. Even though today's meeting was later than usual, already I had to strain to see the path. A thick layer of wet fog descended quickly, compounding the problem. Victor's house was just a shadow, the lights inside twinkling through the mist. From a distance, it reminded me of a huge cruise ship in port, poised and waiting for its next ocean jaunt.

I bounded up the stairs anxious to absorb whatever Victor had to share today. Henry opened the door before I could knock. "Good evening, sir." He smiled his usual Henry smile but looked different tonight, older perhaps. *Probably the lighting,* I thought.

"You seem tired, Henry."

"Oh no, sir. Just adjusting to the darkness so early in the evening. Throws the internal time clock off a bit I'm afraid."

I'd developed a certain affection for Henry over the last several months. I followed him down the massive but familiar hallway. Our footsteps echoed louder than usual. I stopped at the door to the den, but Henry walked right past it. I paused and then reluctantly followed him further down the hall. "Uh, we're not in the den this afternoon?" I asked, confused.

"You've graduated to the study." He smiled. "Mr. Guise is temporarily detained for a few moments. Please make yourself comfortable and I'll be back with some —"

"Strawberry lemonade?" I asked hopefully.

"Yes, sir. Strawberry lemonade coming right up!" I sensed he was pleased with the earnestness of my request.

I settled into a large nicely broken-in leather chair facing the fireplace. The fire was perfect and gave off just the right amount of heat. Henry must have started it shortly before I arrived. The logs glowed orange and popped occasionally. The chair I chose nearly swallowed me when I dropped into it and was so comfortable I hoped I wouldn't fall asleep.

I glanced around the study. It had Victor written all over it. There was no doubt I was sitting in a man cave but one that screamed class and sophistication. No dead animal heads or football jerseys on the walls here, and I couldn't find a single Trappist beer keg in any corner. There was a huge flat-screen TV mounted in an expensive wooden picture frame above the fireplace. It was kind of creepy and kind of cool at the same time. I fully expected the visions of Nostradamus or something equally disturbing to suddenly appear in the framed blackness and totally freak me out.

The walls on both sides of the fireplace were floor-to-ceiling windows, and there was a small bar in the corner. Another sprawling desk like the one in the den was perched behind me and behind it, a wall of books.

Henry returned and poured me a large glass of strawberry lemonade, which I gulped down immediately. He refilled my glass and poured one for Victor. He carefully set the tray with a half-full pitcher on the desk and left me alone in the man cave.

I sat mesmerized by the fire for several minutes before I heard Victor's familiar voice behind me. "Well, hello, Luke! I'm sorry to keep you waiting."

"Not a problem, sir."

"How are you this week?" he asked with genuine interest. "Were you able to spend any time on LinkedIn?"

"I spent my 60 minutes. Time does fly on the Internet, but I added my conditioning phrase to my profile and sent out a bunch of connection notices. I noticed you responded to yours promptly."

"Indeed I did." He smiled.

"So what nuggets of knowledge are you going to share with me today?"

"Ah, I'm glad you asked. We've built systems for some of the more important aspects of your business. Now we have to keep you honest."

Victor sunk deep into the leather chair next to me. I wasn't sure where he was going with this. I sipped my lemonade slowly and gazed into the fire. "So what does that mean exactly?"

"Tracking," he replied, his eyes glued to the fire.

"You mean like assets and revenue? I do that, and so does the firm." I made no attempt to hide my lack of enthusiasm for the topic.

What started as mild amusement morphed into a full smile as he turned to face me, "No, not assets and revenue. Those are the results of your activity. If enough of the right activities are happening on a daily basis, it's only a matter of time before the assets and revenue follow. Would you agree?"

"I guess that's true." I shrugged. "Tracking is good when you're new in the business and you don't know what you're doing. I agree with that, but I think when you've been in the business awhile, it's not as important. It takes time to do, and I'm not sure the value it adds really justifies the extra time."

He cocked his head to one side and studied me for several seconds before asking, "How many client calls did you make today?"

I shifted uncomfortably in my comfortable chair and tried to remember exactly who I had called that day. I counted and recounted silently. Was it possible I'd only called three clients today? Surely, it had to be more than that.

"Uh, I don't know for sure. I'm thinking probably less than 10," I answered vaguely, avoiding his penetrating blue eyes.

"What about prospect calls?"

I knew for sure I hadn't made any of those. If I counted calling to confirm the venue for my next event, that was — well, one. I just shrugged and stared into the fire.

"Luke, my boy. How can you win the game long-term if you don't know the score on a day-to-day basis?" He didn't wait for an answer before continuing, "Football season is coming to a close soon. Who's your favorite quarterback?"

"Well, I drafted Drew Brees for my fantasy football team. So I guess he's my favorite."

"All right. How effective do you think Mr. Brees would be if he was forced to play the entire game with no idea what the score was? Do you think that might distract him from having his best game? And how effective would the rest of the team be?"

"I never really thought about it before, but I doubt he would have his best game," I replied.

"Of course he wouldn't, and the same is true for you. In order to grow your business consistently and systematically, you must know what you're *actually* doing on a day-to-day basis. What advisors think they're doing and what they're actually doing are often two completely different entities."

"You're right about that," I sighed, beating myself up one last time for failing to make more than three client calls today. *Enough of that,* I thought as I pulled out my notebook and Victor pen.

Opening and closing my writing hand several times, I stretched and was ready to write. I inhaled deeply and let my breath out slowly. Closing my eyes, I tried to clear my mind. I'd been practicing the whole yoga mind-clearing thing as part of my success ritual for several weeks now. After several seconds, I could feel my body relax. Prepared for another writing marathon, I opened my eyes and asked, "So what specific activities should I track?"

"First of all, you want to track only activities that you have direct control over. For instance, instead of tracking your total number of calls per day, track your outgoing client calls and outgoing prospect calls. The number of outgoing calls you make in a day is something you directly control."

"I guess I should put all this tracking stuff in an Excel spreadsheet," I said more to myself than to Victor.

"That's what I would suggest. Henry will include a sample spreadsheet in your packet. I would also suggest that you separate client calls from prospect calls so that you become very clear on exactly how much or how little time you're spending on developing new business. You may choose to define a prospecting call differently, but I would define it as any call related to the development of new business."

"You mean calling to secure a venue for my next event would count as a prospecting call?" I asked, hoping my one prospect-related call would be validated.

"This is your tracking system, Luke. You decide what tasks to track, the criteria you'll use to determine what counts as a task and what doesn't, as well as your weekly goals for each task. From a logistical perspective, you must decide the easiest way to implement your tracking system so it becomes a real tool in your business, rather than just another item on a to-do list."

"Tasks, criteria, goals, and implementation. Got it," I said as I scribbled in my notebook.

"So given the nature of your business, what other tasks do you feel you should be tracking? Remember the 80/20 rule. What 20% of your tasks are responsible for 80% of your results?"

"Appointments," I answered without even thinking. "When I have an appointment, it's pretty much a given that I'll generate additional revenue."

"Then it sounds like appointments are definitely one of your results-oriented tasks, and they're also something you control. It's important that you track how many appointments you set each week as well as how many appointments you hold each week."

"But won't that be tracking the same thing twice? I mean the appointments I set this week are going to be the appointments I hold next week."

"A successful appointment is essentially the result of a two-part process," said Victor, "calling to set the appointment and then holding the appointment. The process could break down at either point. Tracking both components gives you more clarity. It's important that you track each component so you can determine the weak link."

"I guess it would also give me a good idea of what my averages are in each area," I added.

"Precisely. Suppose you average five appointments a week, and then one week you realize you only have two appointments. Is that because you failed to set five appointments, or did you actually set five but only two showed up?"

"Hmm. That makes sense." In my notebook I added "appointments set" and "appointments held" to my list of tasks to track.

Victor suddenly rose and walked over to a big brass box next to the fireplace. He rummaged through the stack of split firewood, searching for the perfect log to revive the dying fire. When he found his chosen log, he tossed it onto the glowing embers and grabbed a heavy black poker. He played with the fire for several minutes before it regained its former majesty. Satisfied, he stretched and then dropped back into his chair. It didn't take long before we both fell under the fire's hypnotic spell.

I'm not sure how long we sat in silence. I finally tore myself away from the fire and asked, "So I guess I'd also track things like Referral Detective Entries, my to-do list, extras, stuff like that, right?"

Still focused on the fire, he replied, "Absolutely. However, it would be wise to track all four components of your referral process. In addition to Referral Detective entries, you should track referral letters sent, how many times each week you take a client through the Referral Process Explained, and how many times each week you use the 'you probably can't think of anyone right now' referral conditioning phrase."

"I can do that. What else should I track?" I asked.

"What other tasks do you consider your primary results-oriented tasks?"

"Well, I do quite a bit of networking. I mean not with specific networking groups, but when I'm on the golf course or sailing, I usually consider those networking activities. Also, I think my college alumni association and groups I support, like the Humane Society, are networking opportunities as well."

"Indeed they are," he replied, turning away from the fire to look at me.

"So how would I track that?"

"Remember you want to track the activity, not the results. So what do you think would be the best measure of networking activity?"

I shrugged. "Hours, I guess."

"Very good," he said. "What other results-oriented activities would you be wise to track?"

I considered his question. "I think I'd like to start tracking what I do with LinkedIn. I should probably track connections added, prospects identified, and LinkedIn lunches scheduled and held."

"You're thinking like a real businessman now, Luke."

"Thank you, sir." I knew this was the ultimate compliment coming from Victor.

"Now that you know what specific tasks you're going to track, it's important to consider your weekly goals for each task and include those on your spreadsheet as well. See to it that your goals are a stretch but achievable. "

"There'll probably be some trial and error involved with setting stretch goals that are realistic, especially since I haven't tracked anything since I was a rookie." I chuckled.

"That's to be expected. It is a process after all."

I stared back into the fire. It looked neglected and in need of attention. "Do you mind?" I asked as I reached for the poker.

"By all means," he said with a smile. "Can't keep a man from his fire!"

I shuffled and poked at the log he'd thrown on the dying embers. Finally, it seemed to take a deep breath and exhale new flames. I thought about the tracking spreadsheet and how exactly I could use it most effectively. Finally I broke the silence. "So I guess what I'll do is print the spreadsheet out and keep track of what I do during the day. Then I'll add up my numbers and put them on the spreadsheet on my computer before I leave."

"The logistics of how you use the spreadsheet is a matter of personal preference," he replied. "Your proposed method would likely be the most efficient and accurate way of doing it—*if* you take the time to transfer your numbers to the electronic version at the end of each day."

"I thought about that, and I think I'll just make that part of my to-do list time block. That way I won't forget. It'll also give me a chance to review what I did for the day and make adjustments to the next day's to-do list if necessary."

"Excellent idea."

"So if I have weekly goals for each task on the spreadsheet, I guess I should review the spreadsheet weekly in addition to daily?"

"Correct. The sample spreadsheet that's in your packet is set up to automatically compute your weekly numbers based on each day's accomplishments. I suggest as part of your Friday cleanup block you allocate some time to an 'End-of-the-Week Critique.'"

"Okay. But what is that exactly?"

"It's simply where you review your numbers for each task relative to your goals for the week. It gives you a snapshot of what you *actually* accomplished for the week. Remember, often what advisors think they're doing and what they're actually doing are two completely different things. The spreadsheet and your 'End-of-the-Week Critique' will keep you functioning on reality rather than fantasy."

I laughed. "And that's a good thing?"

"Indeed it is." He chuckled. "In the beginning, you'll want to evaluate whether your goals are reasonable or if they should be modified up or down. If you accomplished your goals for the week, reward yourself. If you didn't, ask yourself why. This helps you determine exactly what needs to change in the upcoming week. In that respect, the 'End-of-the-Week Critique' serves as a preliminary planning tool in setting your agenda for the upcoming week."

"All this tracking stuff makes me realize that I've basically been operating blind for a long time," I said, shaking my head. "Over the last 10 years, the only goals I ever really tracked were production and asset goals."

"That's not uncommon in the business. It's like being a marathon runner who wants to improve his finish time in the next race yet only tracks previous race times. Although that's useful information, in order to make significant improvement, the runner needs to log how many hours he runs, along with his times on a weekly basis. His race times are a result of the running activities he does each week leading up to the race."

"That makes sense. It's going to be a definite shift in focus, but I can see how you would feel less stress and more satisfaction tracking activity instead of obsessing over production and asset numbers constantly."

Victor nodded in agreement. "You feel less stress and more satisfaction because you're tracking what you control. After the first month, you'll want to determine if the goals you established are robust enough to move your business forward in the way you'd like."

"So that means I'll be doing an 'End-of-the-Month Critique' as well?"

"Exactly. If you follow your tracking system consistently, your activity numbers can't help but go up because you're paying attention to them on a weekly, monthly, and even quarterly basis. As you would expect, when those activity numbers go up, your production and assets numbers can't help but go up as well."

"I see how that would work. It seems so obvious — a real

back-to-basics step."

"Basics are basics for a reason, my boy." Victor smiled, his attention drifting back to the fire.

His words were as simple as they were profound. "It's funny how the longer you're in the business, the further away from basics you get—like you don't need them anymore."

Still captivated by the aging fire, he responded in an almost grandfatherly tone, "Oh, I think that's true of most anything we become comfortable with. We just need to be reminded every now and again."

I studied Victor as he watched the fire. He had a powerful yet peaceful presence that was unmistakable. His coaching had radically changed my business and changed me in the process. I felt different—calmer and more in control.

The systems he'd given me were working—and working better than I ever dreamed possible. I believed in them, and with that belief came a quiet confidence I'd never experienced before in the business. I was happier, my family was happier, and so were my clients.

I wanted to keep coming to see him. I knew there was still so much I could learn from him. I wanted Aimee to meet him too. She heard me talk about him all the time, and she'd witnessed firsthand what he'd done for my business—for me.

I wondered how he spent his days. He seemed to have contacts all over the world judging from the bits of conversation I'd overheard periodically when he was on the phone.

I was so deep in thought, I didn't even notice Henry had snuck into the study. He stood quietly waiting, packet in hand. I knew our time today was done. I rose and shook Victor's hand. "Thank you, sir. I think this tracking thing *is* going to keep me honest."

"Indeed it will." Victor smiled.

"See you next week," I said, reluctantly leaving the glowing warmth of the fire. Henry handed me the familiar yellow packet.

"Luke!" Victor called as I headed out the door.

I turned and glanced back at him. "Yes, sir?"

"You've come a long way. I'm proud of you."

I grinned like a kid. He'd finally said it—the words I longed to hear for so long. He was proud of me, and that made me proud.

"Thank you, sir."

I paused and then followed Henry out of the study.

CHAPTER TO-DO LIST

1. Develop your own tracking spreadsheet to monitor progress on weekly goals.

    •   Track only the activities that you control.

    •   Decide on which results-oriented activities you will track.

    •   Determine what criteria you will use to define specific tasks.

    •   Determine what your weekly goals will be for each task you will track.

    •   See a sample spreadsheet by clicking on the link in the Additional Resources section.

    •   Decide on your implementation strategy for using the tracking spreadsheet effectively every day.

    •   Record your results each day as a component of your to-do list time block.

2. Do an "End-of-the-Week Critique" every Friday as part of your Friday Cleanup Time Block.

    •   Use your results as a planning tool in setting the following week's agenda.

For Additional Resources, go to:

**www.executivetransformations.com/
plateau2pinnacle-additionalresources**

11. PUTTING IT ALL TOGETHER

"We make a living by what we get; we make a life by what we give."

— Sir Winston Churchill

I was on top of the world! Everything had come together this week. I'd even blown through my high goal — that pie-in-the-sky goal advisors always set for themselves in the beginning of the year knowing there's not a chance in hell they'll get there. I was up 37% from last year with most of that surge coming in this last quarter of the year. And when I analyzed the numbers, I'd done it without any huge tickets that artificially inflated the growth percentage. I could feel that million-dollar producer award in my hands this time next year.

After my last meeting with Victor, I'd been surprised to find a review exercise in my packet that he hadn't mentioned in our last meeting. He'd included a note telling me to review my progress in everything I'd done since we'd started. I hadn't thought to do this before since I'd been so focused on implementing all of his advice and systems, but as usual,

Victor was right. Going through all of my progress thus far made me realize just how far I'd come.

The client contact schedule alone had made a huge difference in my business. I'd also become an expert at Referral Detective, and it was starting to drive my business in a big way. In fact, in this last quarter I opened more new accounts than I had in the first three quarters combined, and they were substantial accounts too. I was starting to realize that birds of a feather really do flock together!

I'd run my financial plans from last week, and each one seemed to get a little easier and quicker to do. When I presented them, I'd followed Victor's instructions to the letter. Rebecca and both couples were all thrilled with the process. They even agreed to move into my new discretionary platform without the slightest hesitation. Victor had been right there too. They'd thought I already had the ability to make changes to their accounts as necessary and actually seemed relieved that now I could.

What was even more amazing was in all three cases, I thought I had all their money. And in all three cases I was wrong. One of the couples agreed to move another million to me that I didn't even know existed!

The branding was evidently working too. I'd become diligent about using my conditioning phrase every chance I could. In fact, I'd made a game out of it, seeing how many times I could use it in a day. This week I'd had a referral from one of my larger clients come in for an appointment. He recited my conditioning phrase almost verbatim, explaining that's why he'd decided to come in and see me. I couldn't believe it!

Although I'd been highly skeptical at first, I woke up earlier than I ever had before and practiced my success ritual every morning. The meditation was even getting easier and judging from this last quarter, maybe even working. Most mornings I woke up even before Aimee just to have a few extra minutes of silence before the day started.

For the first time in my career, I felt like I wasn't winging it and my destiny was in my hands. No longer did I feel like my success depended on the decisions or whims of clients or prospects. I guess when it came right down to it, I felt proactive — in control.

It was almost Christmas, and I hadn't told Aimee yet, but there was absolutely no doubt in my mind that next year I'd be a million-dollar producer. The foundation had been laid and laid by a master craftsman. Just like Joe, I'd done all the work, but it was Victor who'd made it happen. It would be a stretch, but I knew I could do it. That had been a bucket-list item for me since day 1 in the business, and this time next year, I knew I'd be scratching it off the list.

I couldn't wait to report all of my good news to Victor. I parked in my usual spot and grabbed my briefcase. As soon as I got out of the car, something felt strange. I hesitated and scanned the area before slowly starting up the gravel pathway to the house. I climbed the steps to the huge wraparound porch just like I did every week.

Then I saw it. A small gold envelope was taped to the thick beveled glass on the door. My name was neatly printed on the front. I froze, not able or willing to take a step forward. Joe's words flashed through my mind. Each time Victor had set him up — first with the job at Grayson and then in his own business, he hadn't seen or heard from him for years after. I prayed my time with Victor wasn't over. It couldn't be. I didn't want it to be.

How long I stood there staring at the little gold envelope on the door, I don't know. Finally, I yanked it from the door and peered through the glass. The house was empty, and my heart sank. I flopped down on the stairs. My finger mindlessly traced my name on the front of the envelope. Then I turned it over and opened it carefully.

I took a deep breath and pulled out the gold card inside. I slowly read the handwritten words.

Luke,

I assume by now, you have completed the review process assignment in your packet. Now you see what I've seen from the moment I met you—your infinite potential. To see it, believe it, and to act on it daily is a gift. Use your gift wisely.

And now, we've come to the final and most important assignment you have until the time we meet again. It is my hope that you will be as diligent with this one as you have been with all the others. I'm proud of you, Luke. Now is your time!

PAY IT FORWARD

Victor ∞

"And *that* was my real turning point where everything just came together." I stared out the window and realized my true defining moment had arrived. I'd fulfilled my final commitment to Victor. I was paying it forward.

"Wow," said Randy. "And you never saw him again?"

"Not yet at least. But I do get a birthday card from him every year."

"You think you ever will? See him again, I mean."

"Right now, I'm sure he's off doing deals somewhere and changing lives in the process. But when I'm ready, he'll be back. I'm sure of it. Just like he was for Joe," I answered. And I believed it.

"That was an amazing story, Luke. That could be a movie or something! Thanks so much for sharing it with me, man. I really appreciate it."

I gazed at the kid sitting in front of me and saw that spark Victor had spoken of—the one that had the ability to ignite infinite potential. I knew my decision was a good one.

I smiled and said, "The privilege was mine. Randy, there's

a reason I shared my story with you now." I paused and then continued, "I see *your* potential, and I figured it was time you had a turning point."

"Gee, thanks, Luke. That means a lot coming from you." He blushed.

I knew he didn't really understand. I opened my drawer and pulled out a thick spiral bound book with a ∞ on its gold cover. I slid it across my desk.

"Use your knowledge wisely, my boy."

GETTING ORGANIZED

1. Develop your own Morning Success Ritual. Do what you know will work best in preparing you for a successful day. Some suggestions are:

    *   Meditation

    *   Writing down the day's big-picture goals — the "what" of your day

    *   Visualization — use as many senses as possible to make it real

    *   Exercise — not intended to be your full exercise program but rather something to get you moving and your blood pumping for the day

2. To-do List Rules

    *   Your to-do list must be done before you leave the office for the next day. Establish a time block for it in the afternoon.

    *   Prioritize it. Remember the 80/20 rule applies to your tasks as well as your revenue.

        ➢   A tasks must be done — phone calls and appointments

        ➢   B tasks should be done and delegated whenever possible — research, proposals, market prep

> ➢ C tasks would be nice if they got done — cleaning off desk, reading *WSJ*

> ➢ You cannot move on to B tasks until A tasks are completed, and you cannot move on to C tasks until B tasks are completed. The only exception is if you're waiting on a call back from someone.

> ➢ Call Clients is not a legitimate A task. An example of a legitimate A task is Call Clients with a list of clients to be called and a brief note as to what you will talk to each one about.

3. Begin your time blocking with a 30- to 45-minute block in the morning for calling and one in the afternoon for your prioritized to-do list.

    •   Time blocks are appointments with yourself and should be treated accordingly — schedule around them whenever possible, door should be closed, phone should be on Do Not Disturb, alert your assistant that you are not to be disturbed except for emergencies or market-sensitive calls.

    •   Add to your time block in 15-minute increments and only after you have consistently adhered to your AM and PM time block for five consecutive days.

    •   Only add an additional time block after you have adhered to your existing time blocks consistently for one full production month.

    •   Time blocks are a commitment, so only add additional ones when you have a good reason for doing so.

- Integrate your time blocks into your to-do list until they are a habit.

- No time blocks should be over 60 minutes in length—the chances of you adhering long term to a time block of over 60 minutes are slim.

4. Remember your to-do list and your time blocking add structure to how you operate on a daily basis. Together, they will add to your effectiveness exponentially and therefore have the potential to increase your referrals, assets, and revenue.

PREPARE TO LEVERAGE

1. Segment book by tier.

   - Begin with quantitative analysis using assets and revenue, and assign points accordingly.

   - Change the breakpoints as necessary based on the nature of your book but maintain the same number of breakpoints and the same number of points per breakpoint.

   - Assign points based on intangibles.

   - Total points and assign tiers.

   - Segment using A, B+, B, C, and D tiers.

2. Segment book by age.

   - Over 80

   - 66–79

   - 50–65

   - 40–49

   - Under 40

3. Segment book demographically.

   - Look for common denominators and anomalies.

   - Identify niches within the book.

     ➢ Hobbies

     ➢ Neighborhoods

THE ART OF LEVERAGE

1. Create your own client contact schedule by tier and laminate.

    - Start by being a student of your own behavior and what you're currently doing in the way of client service.

        ➢ What do you want to do more of and less of in the way of client service?

    - Develop a client service model that raises your current level of service and is sustainable.

    - It should be personalized to fit you and your book.

    - If you have a capable assistant, include him or her in some simple client service touches.

    - Delegate whenever possible to leverage your time as well as your book.

    - Include extras — the little things that make a big difference to clients.

    - Always treat A and B+ clients the same in terms of client service.

    - Both you and your assistant should have a laminated copy on your desk and refer to it often.

    - In order for touches to clients to count, they must be proactive and in your control.

2. Develop a Soft Touch Questionnaire (STQ).

    •   Plan on pulling one or two questions to work into conversations with clients.

        ➢   This allows you to increase your level of service by knowing your client better.

        ➢   This allows you to be in a better position to send extras to clients regularly

    •   Keep your STQ handy at all times so you remember to use it.

        ➢   Attach it to the client file in your contact management system with some sort of reminder to pull it up when talking to clients.

        ➢   If you prefer hard copies, use a binder set up alphabetically with an STQ sheet for each client. Keep on your desk at all times with some sort of reminder to use.

3. Automate your client contact schedule.

    •   Start with your A and B+ clients and make your initial phone call.

        ➢   Voice mails count because they are proactive on your part regardless of whether you receive a callback from the client.

        ➢   Have your assistant set all recurring activities from that initial contact so your contacts are staggered.

4. Implement flawlessly.

- Establish a cleanup block on Thursday or Friday for all the contacts and touches that were not made during the week for whatever reason.

- Make it your goal to begin each week with little or no carryover from the previous week.

REFERRALS

1. Use the **12-Minute Tip** to implement changes flaw-
    lessly and consistently.

2. Use the **Referral Detective Strategy**© every single
    day.

    *   Get your **Referral Detective Notebook** — a pock-
        et-calendar-sized or checkbook-sized notebook
        with blank pages.

    *   Each entry should have the date of the conver-
        sation, the source and notes about the entry. A
        proper name is not necessary.

    *   Entries can come from anyone, not just clients.

    *   Use the **7-Second Scan**.

    *   Use **Bait Questions** to generate entries.

    *   Average two entries per day five days a week.

    *   Avoid making judgment calls on the quality of
        entries until you develop your **Referral Detec-
        tive Hit List**.

    *   Develop your Referral Detective Hit List based
        on the quality of the source and notes on the en-
        try.

    *   How you handle the next step — social vs. pure
        business — depends on your style as an advisor
        and the personality of the source.

- Always notice and take advantage of opportunities to condition your clients for referrals.

- Separate the entry from the source as early as possible.

- When holding events, always cross-reference your invitation list with your Referral Detective Notebook for possible entries to have clients bring with them.

3. Use the **Referral Process Explained** once a year, preferably in the first quarter with clients you wish to duplicate.

4. Use the "You probably can't think of anyone right now" sentence once a day to condition at least one client per day to think in terms of referrals.

5. Send a referral letter once a year to clients you wish to duplicate.

BRANDING

1. Develop a powerful elevator speech using the six criteria outlined in the chapter.

    -   Start with one sentence that serves as the hook. It should be mysterious enough to spark questions.

    -   It should have two or three short, concise bullet points to clarify your process.

        ➢ What do you want them to most remember about you?

        ➢ What makes you unique?

    -   It should make prospects question their own situation and plant a seed that they may need you.

    -   You must practice it every day while shaving or putting on your makeup. Use different intonations and try emphasizing different words. Practice until it's as comfortable as saying your name.

    -   End with a hot-button question that gives you a reason to contact the prospect in the future. Always remain calm and casual regardless of their answer.

2. Develop your primary conditioning phrase from your elevator speech.

    -   Include your primary conditioning phrase in a tagline in your e-mail signature.

- Use your primary conditioning phrase in everything you do — every conversation, every meeting, and every piece of correspondence.

- If you write handwritten notes, take your stationery or notecards to a printer and have your conditioning phrase professionally printed at the bottom.

THE POWER OF THE PLAN

1. Build your business model around Financial Planning.

   • A comprehensive financial plan takes the client's focus off of performance and short-term volatility and puts it on the plan.

   • It gives the client peace of mind knowing there is a process at work rather than what may appear to be a random approach to their finances.

   • It allows the advisor to see where all the assets are and to make decisions based on the client's complete financial picture rather than being forced to take a piecemeal approach to their finances.

2. Evaluate your discovery process.

   • Don't shortchange the subjective questioning.

   • Subjective questioning gives insight as to what's really important to the client and is valuable if and when adjustments must be made.

   • Review Henry's list of subjective questions on the website.

3. Modulize.

   • Decide which areas you feel are most important to a comprehensive planning process.

- Develop a list of your modules with a brief synopsis of each and submit to Compliance for approval.

- Laminate your module list and give to the client.

- Present one to two modules per year depending on the client's timing and circumstances.

- Develop a spreadsheet to keep track of where clients are in your process.

- Keep a separate spreadsheet for each client and enter the date and notes each time you complete a module for the client.

THE INVESTMENT MANAGEMENT PROCESS

1. Reread the Case for Discretionary Platforms.

2. Build your Investment Matrix.

   • Pick two primary holdings in the primary style boxes — Large Cap, Mid Cap, Small Cap — Value, Growth, and Balanced in each.

   • Pick two backup holdings in each primary style box.

   • Pick primary investments in the secondary style boxes — REITs, managed futures, alternatives.

   • Pick primary investments in satellite styles — sector funds, international.

3. Build your Platform Model.

   • Establish your breakpoints for small, mid, and large accounts.

   • Decide what platforms you will use for each tier of account.

4. Build your Risk-based Model Portfolios.

   • Create your asset allocation models for each risk profile.

- Build your model portfolios by using the managers within your Investment Matrix to implement your asset allocation models.

5. Build your Pricing Matrix.

- It should be fair to the client and an accurate reflection of the value you bring to the client.

- Develop conviction that you are worth every penny and be worth every penny.

6. Implementation

- Use your discretionary business model with all new clients without exception.

- Existing clients

  ➢ Begin with IRAs — no tax consequences

  ➢ Taxable accounts with little or no tax consequences

  ➢ Taxable accounts with significant tax consequences

    ▪ Move to your discretionary platform immediately.

    ▪ Move toward your models as you can as it makes sense to the client through tax selling and other appropriate strategies.

REVOLUTIONARY PROSPECTING

1. Your LinkedIn profile

    •   Build or update your profile to include your conditioning phrase—display it prominently and preferably more than once.

    •   Be sure there is a link from your profile to your website.

    •   Always use a professional photograph.

2. Using LinkedIn to acquire old-fashioned introductions

    •   Allocate a specific amount of time to Linked-In each week—the amount of time you allocate is dependent on how active you will be in using the site for gaining introductions.

    •   Plan on a minimum of 45–60 minutes each week.

        ➢   Begin by adding a substantial number of connections.

        ➢   Once you've built your number of connections, each week, review your connections' connections or your second-degree connections.

        ➢   Determine your criteria for identifying potential introductions.

            ▪   Professionals

- Individuals in upper and middle management positions

- Individuals who have worked for the same company for many years

- Individuals who work for a company that employs several of your current clients

- Individuals who recently left a company after being employed for many years

- Small business owners

- Individuals who enjoy expensive hobbies — sailing, golf, etc.

➢ Set one LinkedIn lunch per week with one of your connections.

- Bring a list of four to six of their connections you'd like to review with them for potential introductions.

- Begin by discussing their LinkedIn experience and their connections in general terms.

- Review the list with them.

- Put your connection in an advisory role on how best to reach a potential introduction.

- When you receive positive feedback on a certain individual, ask for the introduction but offer them options on how best to reach that individual.

o   Lunch with both your connection and their connection

o   Phone call using your connection's name

o   Invitation for both to your next event

o   LinkedIn introduction

3. Keeping expectations in line with reality.

-   LinkedIn is a revolutionary prospecting tool but not a magic bullet.

-   Be prepared for responses such as the following:

    ➢   They don't know how they ended up on LinkedIn.

    ➢   They don't know the connection you're referencing.

    ➢   They don't know the person you're referencing, but they'll give you the names of some people you should call.

    ➢   The person you're referencing doesn't have any money.

    ➢   The person you're referencing is not someone you'd want to work with.

    ➢   The person you're referencing is someone you should talk to.

4. Develop a structured drip process for all prospects regardless of their origin.

    -   The foundation of the drip should be on autopilot.

        ➤   Use firm-sponsored or outside e-newsletter service to have an e-newsletter sent automatically to all clients and prospects.

        ➤   An e-newsletter cannot be your first contact with someone.

    -   If the prospect is not hot or does not have any perceived immediate potential, call every six to eight weeks.

    -   Mix up your calls.

        ➤   Goodwill/Check-in calls

        ➤   Holiday calls to build rapport

        ➤   Provide information on a particular concern of theirs.

        ➤   Invite to an event or outing

        ➤   Primary objectives for prospecting calls

            -   Come away with a legitimate reason for calling them again.

            -   Make each consecutive call warmer by building rapport—goodwill, check-in, holiday calls.

TRACKING

1. Develop your own tracking spreadsheet to monitor progress on weekly goals.

   • Track only the activities that you control.

   • Decide on which results-oriented activities you will track.

   • Determine what criteria you will use to define specific tasks.

   • Determine what your weekly goals will be for each task you will track.

   • See the sample spreadsheet under "Additional Resources."

   • Decide on your implementation strategy for using the tracking spreadsheet effectively every day.

   • Record your results each day as a component of your to-do list time block.

2. Do an "End-of-the-Week Critique" every Friday as part of your Friday Cleanup Time Block.

   • Use your results as a planning tool in setting the following week's agenda.

ADDITIONAL RESOURCES

The Chapter To-Do List at the end of every chapter was the key component contained in each of Henry's packets to Luke. They were designed to give a step-by-step process for building the system outlined in each chapter. For a complete reference, a compilation of the Chapter To-Do Lists appears in the Putting It All Together chapter.

In addition to the process for building each system, Henry also included some other key tools and resources in Luke's packets. Most of these additional resources can be found on the Executive Transformations website on the dedicated *Plateau to Pinnacle* page. These additional resources are listed by chapter for easy reference and can be found by going to:

**www.executivetransformations.com/
plateau2pinnacle-additionalresources**

It's never too early or too late to begin to develop these systems for your business. Taking the time to work *on* your business and develop the systems in the book can make working *in* your business far more profitable. To receive regular tips and additional resources for building and implementing your systems, subscribe to the Plateau to Pinnacle e-newsletter.

Executive Transformations was founded by Erin Tamberella in 2004. Erin Tamberella and Rick Wright head up the coaching team and have a unique insight that can only come from having sat in the advisor's seat before. They know first-hand not only the challenges a financial advisor faces but also exactly what systems they need to institute in their business in order to be successful long term.

At Executive Transformations, they develop and

build **clearly defined, repeatable systems** for financial advisors that are unique to the individual and designed specifically to forge deeper client relationships. These deeper relationships and the system built around them give the advisor the **power to leverage their existing book for significantly more assets and referrals.**

Good luck in building your systems. Now is the time to **take control of your business and start living your potential.**

ABOUT THE AUTHORS

Erin Tamberella has "sat in the seat" and experienced the daily challenges of a financial advisor firsthand. She spent 17 years as a financial advisor and three years as a producing branch manager.

Originally from New Orleans, she holds a Bachelor of Science degree in Economics from the University of New Orleans. She was Series 7 licensed in August of 1987 and 21 days into her first month of production, she was diagnosed with cancer. Erin spent her first three years in production balancing the challenges of being a rookie with bone marrow biopsies, chemotherapy and radiation.

After beating cancer and excelling in her rookie years, she was ready for a change of scenery. She transferred to the Morgan Stanley branch in Billings, Montana and would later help open the Missoula, Montana branch. She spent 11 years at Morgan Stanley, three of those years as a producing branch manager.

Erin attended the Institute for Professional Empowerment Coaching in Chicago and is a Certified Empowerment Coach. In 2004, she started her financial advisor coaching firm, Executive Transformations, Inc.

In addition to coaching advisors from all over the country, she is also a regular *Horsesmouth* contributor and avid writer. *Plateau to Pinnacle* is her first industry-related book. Her next project is a follow-up business parable for financial advisors.

Rick Wright has spent the last twelve years in the Wealth Management business, including three years as a Producing Branch Manager and four years as a Complex Business Development Officer. During that time, he was instrumental in helping many Financial Advisors build their businesses.

While in his management roles, Rick was instrumental in helping many advisors transition their businesses from other firms to Morgan Stanley. While a Complex Business Development Officer, his complex was consistently ranked in the top five complexes in the country for revenue growth and the top ten percent of the company for asset growth for existing advisors.

Rick graduated with a Bachelor of Science Degree in Computer Science in 1978 and a Master's Degree in Business Administration with an Organizational Behavior focus in 1985; both degrees were from the Florida Institute of Technology in Melbourne, FL. Rick's industry certifications included: Certified Financial Planner, a Chartered Financial Consultant, and a Retirement Income Certified Professional. Rick is a Certified Mastermind Executive Coach through the Executive Coaching University.

Originally from Pennsylvania, Rick's first career was in the technology industry – starting as a software engineer and ultimately becoming President and C.E.O. of two different technology firms. After selling his ownership in the technology firms, Rick and his wife took a two year sabbatical -- cruising the Bahamas and the east coast of the United States on their 48 foot Motor Yacht.

CPSIA information can be obtained at www.ICGtesting.com
Printed in the USA
LVOW10s2056210715

447060LV00001B/189/P